HERE'S EVERYTHING YOU WANT TO KNOW ABOUT

BRAD PITT

His house . . .
It's a turn-of-the-century mansion high up in the Hollywood Hills previously owned by a campy TV horror-show hostess. Secluded behind a green iron gate and dense shrubbery, you'll find out how this hideaway holds most of his very personal secrets.

His lifestyle . . .
From driving like a bat out of hell around Los Angeles to dropping in on Johnny Depp's L.A. Viper Room, does he really have only one thing on his mind (and it's *not* hanging out with the guys)?

His women . . .
It's said he falls in love oh so easily. He's gone with good girls and bad girls, wild sisters and sweet homebodies, but which kind of lady catches his eye . . . and who will be most likely to keep hold of his heart?

His sex appeal . . .
A tall, lanky, blue-eyed blond, he's got one of the hunkiest bodies to hit the silver screen in years. But are those sultry, sensual looks just part of the public role he plays . . . or is he still sexy when the cameras aren't rolling?

BRAD PITT

CHRIS NICKSON

St. Martin's Paperbacks

BRAD PITT

Cover photograph courtesy Rex USA Ltd.

For information address St. Martin's Press, 175 Fifth Avenue, New York, N.Y. 10010.

ISBN: 0-312-95727-0

Printed in the United States of America

St. Martin's Paperbacks edition/October 1995

10 9 8 7 6 5 4 3 2 1

This one's for Graham

Acknowledgments

First of all, my sincere thanks to my agent, Madeleine Morel, for her continuing belief in me. To John Rounds, my editor on this project. To *Movieline* and Paul Benjamin for the fax, and Sarah Weinstein for the call to a friend. And to many of the usual suspects—Dave and Dennis for the television tips, my parents for the clips, the Hornbergs and Watkins for more clips, Dani for the library work overseas, the cats for not letting me get too carried away, and, as always, my wife Linda for putting up with me when I did.

Much here would have been far more difficult without a number of articles as sources, including "Born to be Brad" by Michael Angell in *Movieline,* "A Legend to Fall For" by Pam Lambert and others in *People,* two interviews in *Rolling Stone,* including "Slippin' Around on the Road with Brad Pitt" by Chris Mundy, Fred Schruers's "Tristan The Night Away," which appeared in *Premiere,* "The Bad Boy Makes Good" by Kristine McKenna in the *New York Times,* and Johanna Schneller's interview with Brad in *Vanity Fair*.

Introduction

Brad Pitt has magic.

It's not just the face, although it easily could be. Or the grin, which can make him look as vulnerable as a fourteen-year-old boy. It's not even the body.

Put him on screen and the man creates a spell. A few others have had it—Rudolph Valentino, James Dean, Robert Redford. They come along rarely, but when they do, they imprint themselves on hearts and minds.

Whether he's in a dusty Oklahoma small town, a Montana river, or even a cartoon land, Brad Pitt is capable of doing just that. According to *People* magazine, he's "The Sexiest Man

Alive," and the title has never been so accurately bestowed. The camera loves him, and so do millions of women.

As Julia Ormond, his co-star in *Legends of the Fall,* noted, "I think Brad has something very special. . . . He's not egotistical. He's very, very careful with people—and sweet."

Add to that polite, sensitive, and intelligent, and you have the portrait of a man who has everything going for him. It's hardly any wonder the world's beating a path to his door.

It was his stunning appearance in *Thelma and Louise* that really made the public aware of him, of course. As the sly robber J. D., looking great in a pair of denims—and even better without them—he took Geena Davis's Thelma somewhere she'd never been before, then took her money, while pulses pounded in theaters all across the country. People started asking themselves, "Who *was* that guy?"

It was only some fifteen minutes on-screen, but he made every single second count. Brad Pitt walked onto the set a virtual nobody and came out a rising star.

But although he made his breakthrough as a hearthrob, he refused to be limited by it. As he realized long ago, "Hearthrobs are a dime a dozen."

So, in the year that followed he played a rock 'n' roll wannabe with the ridiculous pompadour of *Johnny Suede,* the upright 'noid cop of *Cool World* and the bright, doomed brother of *A River Runs Through It*. It was quite a range—and that was exactly the point. Having done one thing, and proved himself, it was time to move on to something else. As his mother, Jane Pitt, described him, "He's just someone who's always liked to try new things."

But there's far more to Brad Pitt than meets the eye. There's the man who keeps a sketchbook by his side virtually all the time, and is obsessed with making architectural drawings. Then there's the man who prefers music to movies, with hundreds of CDs and a roomful of guitars and recording equipment in his house, who would still love to be a rock 'n' roll star and can easily join the throng diving into a mosh pit. Or the avid reader, or the guy who just wants to be "out cutting up." And the one who collects antique glass and handcrafted furniture.

They're all the same person, the Brad who approaches his life with a Zen-like attitude of if it feels right for the moment, do it, don't think about it.

It's been the guiding principle of his life, the reason he decided to act, even though he had very little experience, and why he headed west to try his hand in Los Angeles in 1986.

The stardom he achieved wasn't anything he ever sought, but it wasn't something he could fight. He'd been blessed with a natural charisma. Along with his looks and build, it made him an unstoppable force.

"Brad Pitt comes out very well on the screen," judged Phillipe Rousselot, who was the cinematographer on *A River Runs Through It* and *Interview with the Vampire*. "There are some actors who are like that; no matter what light you apply to them, the audience will find them attractive!"

By his own admission, Brad is something of a drifter and a loner. On location he buys a bicycle to allow himself the luxury of slipping away from the madness when he's not needed. When everything's wrapped up, he leaves the bicycle there, locked. If he comes back sometime, well, maybe it'll be waiting for him. . . .

It fits in with that whole way he approaches life. "I'm not leaving anywhere," he said to *Rolling Stone*. "I'm going somewhere."

And it's his acting that's taken Brad everywhere he's been.

"The hardest thing is to make it look easy," he said. But he's managed it remarkably well. The work, the face, the body, the walk, even the life—he's made them all look golden. But while everyone else has only praise for him, Pitt has taken a far more objective view of himself.

"I'm a good actor," he explained. "I'm consistent, but I'll never be a great actor. Every now and then I'll be great. Every now and then I'll be lousy."

Perhaps that's accurate; but perhaps the talent runs deeper than he really thinks. Brad's ability comes more from the heart than from any training, which makes it seem all the more alive. On the set Brad can open himself up, and let the emotions flow straight to the surface.

As he admitted, "You go on instinct, on impulse. You have all these grand theories about your character, but I never really understand them until I see the movie."

Or, as Tom DiCillo, who directed him in *Johnny Suede*, expressed it, "A lot of actors are busy putting up clouds of smoke, but you can see right into him."

And that's a great deal of what makes him so attractive. Not only is he the classically handsome American, muscular and strong featured—"a throwback to what I thought Americans should be like," said Ralph Bakshi, the creator and director of *Cool World*—he's also obviously sensitive, a listener. It's the perfect combination of features.

At thirty-one, he's already achieved a great deal. His name is virtually a household word, his face is pinned up on any number of walls. And in true nineties fashion, he's the subject of a number of computer bulletin boards. He's come to define the romantic star of our time, a mixture of Gable and Redford.

But he's also worked hard to try and be taken seriously as an actor, amassing a body of work that shows a willingness—a desire, really—to constantly stretch and challenge himself, even at the expense of his image.

Yet each one has somehow managed to add

to the legend, which has grown to the point where he can command almost any role he chooses. He's in constant demand, not only for his looks, but also for his skill.

As his stature has risen, so has his price for a film. When *Interview with the Vampire* opened, his fee for a movie was $3 million. Once *Legends of the Fall* became a box-office smash—largely because of his portrayal of Tristan—that figure had doubled.

Even in an industry that's based on manufacturing stars, Brad Pitt is a phenomenon, mostly because he *wasn't* manufactured. He came to it honestly, without hype or a torrent of publicity. And though he's been blessed with talent and a number of physical advantages, the real cause of his success is the traditional virtue of hard work.

And now he's without a doubt the biggest name in the movies, a true idol of the big screen.

But beyond the hoopla, beyond the photographs and the items in the gossip columns, who, exactly, is Brad Pitt? Where did he come from, what makes him tick? And just what is it that makes him so special?

One

William Bradley Pitt came into the world in Shawnee, Oklahoma, on December 18, 1963. It was a time of flux in America. Just a few weeks before, John F. Kennedy had been assassinated, and in a couple of months the Beatles would appear on *The Ed Sullivan Show* and begin the process of social revolution.

For Bill and Jane Pitt, though, all that seemed very far away. The boy was their first child, and they were thrilled with him, with a face so like his father's and a pair of startling blue eyes. From the very beginning Jane, in the way of all mothers, was convinced that her son would be talented, and she kept telling him so, encouraging him in everything he did.

Shawnee was a small town of some twenty-four thousand people (which still made it one of the larger places in the state), located on the North Canadian River, some forty miles east of Oklahoma City and sixty miles southwest of Tulsa. Like all small towns, it placed high values on the family, tradition, and religion, the fabric of American life. The Pitts, firm churchgoing Baptists, were comfortable there; it was, after all, where they'd grown up.

Bill worked as a manager for a trucking company; it was a white-collar job, not always easy, but good, steady employment in an area which had ridden the unsteady booms and busts of the oil business for decades.

All in all, Shawnee was a good place to be then. Nature was close at hand, whether in the state parks or up in the Ozark Mountains, which straddled the borders with Missouri and Arkansas.

The Pitts weren't destined to stay there, however. Soon Bill took a better job which transplanted the three of them over those mountains to Springfield, Missouri.

Geographically, the distance wasn't that great, but in many other ways things were totally different. The accent and the courtly manners might have remained more or less the same, but Springfield was almost four times the size of Shawnee, a bustling, growing city with three colleges. Set in the middle of the Springfield Plain, nestled by the foothills of the Ozarks, it served as the major business center for the surrounding agricultural area.

Which meant that in his new job Bill Pitt was much busier—and better paid. The money soon came in handy, as the family grew. When Brad—as he was soon called to distinguish him from his father—was three, Jane gave birth to another boy, Douglas, then, two years after that, a girl, Julie.

His new employers expected a lot from Bill Pitt. He had a good position, a big improvement over the one he'd enjoyed in Shawnee, but he also had much more responsibility and the position was more demanding.

"I understand that people work," Brad told *Vanity Fair*, "my father spent thirty-six years, six days a week on the job."

It also often took him away from home, leaving the family that meant so much to him for days at a time. But he did his best to make it up to them, taking his children on trips whenever possible, and devoting what little free time he had to them.

There was also the comfort of religion, the backbone of it all. After moving to Springfield, the Pitts began attending South Haven Baptist Church, and once Brad was old enough, he joined the choir, where he quickly made sure everyone's eyes were on him.

"You couldn't keep from watching Brad," accompanist Connie Bilyeu (who would also be his high school drama teacher) remembered, "because his face was so expressive. He would move his little mouth so big with all the words that he attracted everyone's attention."

As Jane described them, the Pitts were a "close-knit" family and remain so even today. The siblings truly loved each other even while they were growing up, as Julie recalled.

"I always looked up to both of my brothers. I just thought they were the greatest things that ever happened. Doug and Brad really play off each other," she said.

Of course, the brothers would rough and tumble together while they were growing up. It was natural; they were boys, competitive and full of energy. But there was never any meanness behind it, and Brad, bigger and older, would stop as soon as Doug yelled "Uncle!"

In many ways it was an ideal home, almost a throwback to the fifties. The family was happy. Bill and Jane weren't overly harsh disciplinarians, but they made sure they instilled basic virtues in their children—politeness, respect, and compassion. It was a very solid grounding for life.

But it was still very much a southern house, with all the male rites of passage associated with the region. As soon as Brad was old enough, his father gave him a BB gun and taught him how to shoot it. Once he'd become thoroughly accustomed to that, Bill allowed him to graduate to a shotgun. It was one of the many parts of his upbringing that's remained in his life: He still keeps the weapon, along with a 12 gauge and a handgun, in his house for protection—and he's willing to use it.

"It's a big deal in Missouri—the way I grew up—to have a gun," he explained to *Rolling Stone*. "And damn right. If someone comes into my house in the middle of the night, I'm going to shoot [them]."

The parents did everything they could to

make sure their children succeeded in school, nurturing talent and building confidence. Brad quickly proved to be an attentive, thorough student, a high achiever in everything he attempted—which was a lot.

By the time he reached Kickapoo High School he'd already achieved a very admirable academic record, and soon he was immersed in any number of extracurricular activities, from sports to student government to choir. A follower of the preppie look that was fashionable at the time, he ended up being voted "Best Dressed Student" in his yearbook, the *Kickapoo Gold*. For a while, as with most boys, baseball was a passion, even if he never showed the talent of a major league player. The game left its mark on him too, in the form of a scar on his left cheekbone, which happened when he lost a fly ball in the sun. But he claimed proudly that he still threw the batter, even with blood streaming down his face.

"Brad was a super kid," remembered Assistant Principal Sandra Grey Wagner, and certainly he was one of those kids teachers love, bright, outgoing, well behaved, and eager, trying everything and excelling. Even so, there were times when, like any pupil, he could try their patience. Like any young man, he had his limits, and one day in his senior year, another kid pushed him past them, and the two started fighting.

"The teacher got involved," he recalled for *Movieline*, "she got her dress ripped. . . . It was over something stupid, I can't even remember. . . . I'm the one who *hit* the teacher, by the way. I know I didn't win, but I didn't get my ass kicked."

Ironically, the one area where his star didn't really shine was in the school plays. He took part in them, even the musicals, but he was never more than a supporting player. Drama didn't seem to particularly absorb him. There was certainly no inkling that he was destined to become one of the best known actors of his generation.

By the time he reached his teens Brad's real interests had become music, art, and films—not for any future possibilities they raised, but for the other worlds they introduced him to, the places beyond Springfield, Missouri.

The Pitts went to movies fairly often, usually to the drive-in, where it was easier to control the three kids. *Butch Cassidy and the*

Sundance Kid was the first film Brad really remembered seeing, when he was six. He liked the action, but it made no real impact on him. *Tommy* was the first movie to do that. He'd already bought the album, by the Who, so he knew the story. But he sat through Ken Russell's epic twice anyway, transported by the magic of the Pinball Wizard.

Then it was *Ordinary People* and *Saturday Night Fever*, and the other big hit movies of the late seventies. But the one that affected him most was quite unexpected.

Like the others, he saw it at the drive-in with the rest of the family. It was a hot summer night, humid and still, so Brad sat on the hood of the car, the family Buick, eating popcorn and drinking Kool-Aid. But as soon as the screen lit up, he forgot everything else.

The film was *Planet of the Apes*, starring Charlton Heston and Roddy McDowall, and it changed his way of looking at the world. Even today, he refers to it often; to the southern teenager, it was profound, an eloquent comment on society and belief.

"I think it's actually very accurate to religion in general today," he reflected years later.

In music, too, he could remember the first

record that really hit him. He'd grown up with rock 'n' roll, it was everywhere on the radio, but it never really spoke to him until he heard Elton John's "Daniel." Then, as with movies, he was lost. He bought the album, *Captain Fantastic,* and was soon discovering other things, even beginning to learn the guitar, wondering if he had the makings of a rock star—something he'd still like to be.

Art nourished another side of him. He'd always drawn, but, unlike most boys he stuck with it, keeping a notepad and a pencil in his pocket to make quick sketches. Like most things he attempted, he was good at it, and it continued to fascinate him, trying to capture lines and expressions on paper.

Church had remained a regular Sunday activity for the Pitts as the children grew. The youngsters didn't resent going; indeed, they were believers themselves, and the routine seemed a perfectly normal slice of life. But even so, Brad couldn't help wanting to deflate the seriousness of it all, the hushed tones and stuffy atmosphere. Even worse, more than anything, he lived in dread of being picked to lead the final prayer.

"I would go into a sweat. . . . I would sit there and say, 'Please, God, not me.' That was my final prayer."

Surprisingly, Brad didn't have an endless stream of dates and girlfriends through his high school years. But he didn't need them; he already had a steady, Sara Hart. She brought out the romantic in him for the first time. It was first love for them both, and he didn't care who knew it. The day after they met at an inter-school debate—Sara didn't attend Kickapoo High—Brad stomped around in the snow outside her classroom window, making a heart and spelling out the words "Hi Sara."

On their first date he took her out to dinner, then home to meet his family. From then on, they were pretty much inseparable, going to the movies every weekend or just staying home and watching television and listening to music. The two of them made one of those couples that seemed to be everywhere together, to the point where a few people wondered if they wouldn't end up getting married. They went to each other's proms. And more than a few girls were jealous of Sara. After all, Brad was the one with everything going for him. Clever and outgoing, he'd inherited his father's good looks and his mother's sweet personality. Blue eyed, already rangily muscular, with blond hair that stopped just short of being long, he was the type of boy a girl could quite easily take home to Mother.

His interest in girls, though, had begun much earlier. By the fourth grade he was already angling for his first relationship—and his first kiss.

"She was the well-developed one. . . ." he said, remembering for *In Style*. "It was in her garage. We actually met there to kiss . . . like we were going to fight or something. It took about a half hour to get to it. And then I ran off."

In junior high he'd dated Kim Bell, his first girlfriend, after getting a friend to call during Christmas vacation to ask if she'd "go with him." She quickly agreed; Brad was a real catch, one of the most popular boys in school. It was sweet, and it lasted for a while. But it wasn't real, more like a pair of kids playing grown-up, rehearsing for what was to come.

Athletic and well coordinated, Brad soon made a name for himself in sports at Kickapoo High. He tried out for everything; as a tennis player, he was good enough to take part in tournaments. It was during one of these that his father (who'd come to watch) offered a piece of advice which would prove pivotal in his son's life.

Brad was throwing a John McEnroe tantrum, tossing his racket and yelling, when Bill Pitt came onto the court in the break between games and asked quite simply if he was having fun. When Brad angrily replied that no, he wasn't, his father just looked into his eyes, said, "Then don't do it," and strolled away.

"Boy, that put me in my place," Brad admitted. "I should have gotten my ass kicked, but he was so above that."

He didn't realize it then, but the words would stay with him, and keep coming back when he needed them.

Once Brad got his driver's license, the family car was passed on to him. It was an old Buick Centurion, the one they used to take to the drive-in, with a big 455 engine, the kind Detroit had stopped making a few years before. "But it was a two-door, so it was just passable enough."

Mobility was important, not just to a teenager but to anyone in that part of the country, with its network of small towns and long, empty stretches of highway. It gave Brad the chance to explore, to drive up into the Ozarks alone and see just how beautiful the region around his home really was.

He'd known the area all his life, since the trips he'd taken with his father, but now he had the chance to see that this was *his* country, the land his people came from, the place that centered him. As much as anything else from those years, that feeling would remain with him, and once he was finally making money in Hollywood, Brad would start buying parcels of land in the mountains, until he'd finally acquired six hundred acres to use as a retreat and a place for family reunions.

There was never any doubt in the family that Brad would go to college upon graduation. His high school record was excellent, he had a good, academic mind behind his laid-back personality, and he loved to read. More than that, it was the accepted next step to success—a good job, a family, and happiness. Certainly he never questioned the rightness of it all. The only question seemed to be, which school should he attend?

Eventually he opted for a college within the state, the University of Missouri at Columbia, some hundred-and-fifty miles from home. The institution, which was founded in 1839, was the oldest state university west of the Mississippi, and big enough to have expanded to three other campuses. The Greek system remained a strongly established part of life there, dominating the social scene; if a freshman wanted to be somebody, he joined a fraternity.

The university also boasted the oldest—and a very well-respected—school of journalism in the country, which could well have influenced Brad's decision, since he'd chosen to major in journalism with a focus on advertising, allowing him to pursue the art he loved.

Unlike so many newer places of higher learning, the University of Missouri had been built on a grand scale. The buildings had a European, almost Gothic air, and the beautifully maintained lawns grounds were eerily dominated at the center of West Campus by five tall columns, the remains of the original administration building, which had been destroyed by a fire in 1892. Among such a scale of work and history, it was impossible for a new student not to feel awed, and for a few weeks Brad was no different.

But, away from home for the first time, free of the moderating influence of his parents, he began to allow himself a little wildness. As was expected of him, he joined a fraternity, Sigma Chi, and moved into the frat house. At that time, at least, Columbia had a reputation among students as a party school, and the fraternity members—including Brad—did their part to live up to it.

"That school kind of revolves around a keg," Brad declared later. "We had this idea of *Animal House,* and there was definitely that aspect. It was a highlight, without a doubt."

But although there were plenty of crazy nights, there was also work. The School of Journalism was grueling, expecting exemplary work from its pupils, and Brad found himself putting in long hours to keep up the grades he'd maintained quite easily in high school.

The change of scene also brought time for serious reflection. For a few years now he'd found himself wondering about religion, how much he believed the things he'd been taught—whether he even believed them at all. Church had been so much a part of his childhood, a given in his life. It had been an anchor for his parents, and for a long time it had been for him, too, keeping him thinking about "higher things."

But, he began to realize, the time had come to let it go, to accept what his heart had been telling him, even at the risk of hurting his mother and father. The truth was, he didn't believe anymore. It was a difficult, in some ways quite devastating decision, to turn his back on a lifetime of acceptance. Still, after a long time of soul-searching, he knew it was the right thing for him.

"One of the most pivotal moments I've had," he said, "was when I finally couldn't buy the religion I grew up with. That was a big deal. It was a relief in a way that I didn't have to believe that anymore, but then I felt alone. It was this thing I was dependent on."

A little emptier and sadder, but wiser and more at peace with himself, Brad moved on. Interestingly, a few years later Bill and Jane Pitt would change themselves, not to reject religion like their son, but to join a nondenominational congregation.

* * *

Brad soon became a familiar face around the college. Muscular, six feet tall, he'd grown fully into his looks and become one of the school hunks—which naturally made him extremely popular with the girls. Since he and Sara Hart, to peoples' surprise, had gone their separate ways after high school, Brad wasn't slow to take advantage of his new status. That popularity received a huge boost when he was asked—and readily agreed—to pose for a campus fund-raising calendar.

It was his first, and, he expected, his last, appearance as a pinup. Bare-chested, grinning, it was obvious even then that the camera liked him, and could light up something in him. Certainly the women at the University of Missouri thought so; the calendar immediately sold out, and for a while Brad became something of a school celebrity, a Big Man on Campus. Everyone knew who he was. Although there was absolutely no way he could he know it at the time, Brad Pitt was getting a very brief, faint glimpse of the future.

His four years of college were, on the whole, a good time, mostly carefree and fun. Once he became used to it, the work wasn't too difficult, and he found he had a flair for writing.

He'd toned down the excesses of his freshman year—as he said, "you grow out of it,"—without lessening any of his enjoyment. There was still time to party, cruise, talk, and have a full social life.

But, at one point, it almost became a very short life.

Brad still had the big Buick that had been handed down to him. He'd never been crazy about the car, but it did have its good points—namely, it hadn't cost him anything, and you could fit plenty of people in it. What he didn't realize was that the things he didn't like about it—its size and weight, and the fact that it was built like a tank—would end up saving his life.

One night, as he told it, out riding in the country around Columbia, "I got hit by an eighteen-wheeler. Not much left of the car. Took the roof with it. Just turned into us and took us with him. No one was even hurt. It was just kind of like once we had a roof and now we don't."

Even years later he still sounded amazed at the whole incident; at the time it was a shattering experience. Brad and his friends had been very lucky. One glance at the roadside, the broken metal in the moonlight and the car roof on the other side of the ditch, and that much was obvious. One moment they'd been joking, the next the windshield was full of light. . . . It was a sharply terrifying reminder that reality could easily intrude on happiness, and that nothing was guaranteed, least of all life itself. It wasn't something they could laugh away.

Once the shock had begun to wear off, Brad replaced the car. He found something new, smaller, sportier, a Nissan he christened "Runaround Sue" after the Dion song from the sixties.

But although one automobile could easily be substituted for another, there was nothing he could do to subdue the thoughts the accident had raised.

To an outsider, even to most of his friends, by his senior year Brad appeared to have the rest of his life mapped out. A degree, a job writing copy with an advertising agency, an eventual promotion to art director. It all seemed so simple. It was certainly the way everyone else was looking at things: a good job, a wife, kids.

The only problem was that Brad began to

realize it all seemed hollow. To settle straight down, take a middle course through life, didn't seem like much of an achievement. All his life he'd been hearing about the outside world, reading about it, seeing it on television and in the movies. It had excited him. Could he just let it go by, only experiencing it on two-week family vacations?

Maybe it was the brush with death that planted the seed, or maybe it was the catalyst for something that had been simmering below the surface much longer. Whatever the reason, as winter turned to spring in 1986, Brad began to realize he wasn't truly happy, and that he couldn't follow the course he thought he'd laid out for himself. He didn't want to become a journalist or an advertising man.

"You keep finding things in little increments," he said, adding later, "finally I realized there was something better."

He also recalled his father's advice—if it's not fun, don't do it. The question was, what *would* he do? Then, finally, out of the blue came the realization he could just walk away. There was nothing tying him there. He could leave Missouri, go wherever he wanted, try to be whatever he desired.

"You don't really get it into your head that you can leave, because . . . I don't know," he tried to explain in 1992. "Not too many people leave. Till it was about time to graduate and it just dawned on me—'I can leave.' It would be so simple."

When he finally understood that, it was as if a huge weight had lifted, as if he was suddenly freer than he'd even been before. It was his life, and he could do whatever he wanted, succeed, fail, anything—it was all up to him.

But where would he go? America was a vast country. There were lots of places for a Missouri boy to find something. Then he remembered the movies that had always fascinated and transported him, and he had his answer. He'd go to Los Angeles and become an actor. It was as simple as that.

"You load up the car, you point it west, and you leave. And everything's open."

So, in May 1986, two credits—a single paper—short of his degree, Brad Pitt amazed his fraternity brothers by loading his possessions into Runaround Sue, waving goodbye to the University of Missouri, and leaving.

Suddenly the future was a big open book.

Two

In some ways he couldn't help feeling like a little kid, the excitement gradually rising as he crossed each state line, and California grew closer. Through Oklahoma, Texas, New Mexico, Arizona, the landscape growing steadily more desolate, and finally the Golden State itself. Then over the San Bernadino mountains and down to the Pacific.

But what, exactly, would be waiting for him there?

Whatever Brad expected Los Angeles to be, it was much more and much less than the picture he'd built up in his mind. Sure, it was far bigger than anywhere he'd seen in Missouri, sprawling mile upon mile through neighborhoods whose names he'd heard for years on television. It was impossible not to keep pulling over and staring.

But by the time he'd reached Burbank the thick smog had brought him back to earth. It settled around him like warm brown fog as he pulled into a McDonald's parking lot. Walking across to the restaurant, he couldn't help but shake his head and wonder, "Shouldn't there be a little more?" and ask himself if he'd made the right decision after all.

No; he'd made his bed, and now, for better or worse, he was determined to lie in it.

He hadn't told his parents exactly what he was doing, of course. There'd been no way to explain it without sounding crazy. How could he say that he was quitting school so close to graduation to follow something that wasn't even really a dream, but just a whim? They wouldn't understand. He wasn't even sure he understood it himself.

So instead he came up with a story that he was traveling west to attend the Art Center College of Design, in Pasadena. It allayed their fears, and it seemed perfectly plausible; studying there could only help him reach that goal of being an art director and set him on a nice, even career path.

They seemed to believe him. His mother even sounded pleased that he was taking it all so seriously. When the phone call was over, Brad put the phone down and sighed. With the family taken care of, now he only had to look after himself. As he soon discovered, savings of $325 didn't go very far in L.A.—a mattress on the floor in an apartment with a bunch of other guys. And as for coming into town with no real acting experience and hoping to land a part, well, that was about as likely as flying to the moon. In most cases, you didn't get roles without an agent, and you didn't get an agent without experience, the classic Catch-22. Any way you looked at it, Brad was on the outside. This might have been the City of Dreams, but bringing those dreams to life wasn't going to be easy.

Still, he wasn't about to let the facts deter him. He'd come out here to make his mark, and he wasn't about to slink home with his tail between his legs at the slightest problem. The first thing he needed was money, to take care of the basics—to pay the rent and put food in his mouth. Since he was broke, that meant taking whatever he could find, just so long as it paid. So, a few days later he was delivering refrigerators to college students, hauling them off the trucks, sweating them up elevators and into dorm rooms. Then, when that job vanished, he tried his hand at telemarketing.

On the surface it didn't sound too difficult. Just turn on the southern accent and the charm to try and sell tickets for a police fund-raiser. But the reality was grinding and soulless. Dialing numbers hour after hour, being hung up on and yelled at—it wasn't worth it. He quit and became a chicken.

El Pollo Loco was a fast-food chain with outlets across Southern California, featuring Mexican food. Brad became their mascot, dressing up as a giant chicken to welcome customers. It was hot, it was definitely sweaty, and it was demeaning, but it helped pay the bills.

And all the time, in between trying to make ends meet, he was attending open auditions, hoping to find some sort of acting job, meeting hundreds of others in exactly the same position. After a couple of months it began to seem discouraging, and Brad set himself a goal—to get a real part in a year. If not . . . well, then he'd have to think again.

There was one brief bright spot, when he was hired to work as an extra in the movie *Less Than Zero*. Standing in a crowded room didn't exactly tax his abilities, but it was a start. He was going to be on-screen, even if it was only for a second or two, and he had the paycheck to prove it.

Brad continued to move around from job to job, always looking to find something that paid just that little bit more, and didn't interfere with his schedule of auditions. He was still convinced he could make it as an actor. Everyone told him he had the looks, and in his heart he believed he had the talent. It needed patience, that was all, and he had that. Even though life could be a bit of a financial struggle, he was having a great time in California.

"At the time," he laughed later, "it was all exciting."

He had no real responsibilities, plenty of new friends, and things were always happening. He still loved music every bit as much as movies, and went out to see bands whenever the opportunity arose. One of the possessions he'd made sure he packed into Runaround Sue was his guitar, and as soon as he found some music buddies in Los Angeles, he was jamming with them, talking about forming a band, still harboring faint dreams of becoming a rock star. But however appealing the ideas sounded, they never became more than that. He needed to concentrate on his acting.

He still hadn't told his parents what he was really doing. He couldn't, not until he'd landed that first real role and could say he'd succeeded, or at least begun. So, on his phone calls home, even while he hated to lie to Bill and Jane, he kept up the pretense of an art course, making up details of nights spent studying.

Meanwhile he was out every evening. Not going to clubs or bars, but in his new position as the driver for girls who delivered strip-o-grams. The work was easy, it paid better than anything he'd done yet, and the girls were fun to be around. Like him, most of them had come west to act, and were just doing what was necessary to survive until their big breaks arrived.

Something Brad didn't have that he really needed was an acting coach, someone to bring him along and refine the rough talent he was certain he possessed. So he was delighted when one of the strippers offered to introduce him to hers. He was good, she said. Maybe he could help.

Roy London is dead now. But in his day, he had an excellent reputation as an acting coach. He'd worked with stars as well as the up-and-coming. And plenty of the novices he trained ended up being able to make more than satisfactory livings in television or movies. Michelle Pfeiffer had studied with him. So did Sharon Stone. Roy London was the man to which Brad was introduced.

However much natural ability Brad possessed, however good he looked, he was still a complete newcomer to the business. London took him in hand, bluntly assessed his strong and weak points, and showed him how to focus what he had and how to present himself.

Brad was a quick learner, a hard worker who was always willing to labor over scenes, monologues, technique, all the pieces of the craft. There was an awful lot to take in, beginning with just simply breathing and standing, two things that seemed perfectly natural but that an actor had to be able to make into art forms.

He progressed rapidly, as if he'd just

needed this as a catalyst to set him in motion. And very soon it paid off, as he got his first break.

The break wasn't a job, but something that would make it a lot easier to get one. A woman in Roy London's class had been able to set up an audition for herself with an agent, and asked Brad to go along with her, and play the male role in the scene she was reading.

In many ways it was one of those classic Hollywood stories, almost a cliché. Brad was there mostly to offer support, trying to keep in the background and maybe learn a little bit more about the business. He spoke his lines and retired. However, when it was all over, it wasn't the woman that the agent wanted to sign, but Brad.

It was a start. An agent was a necessity if you wanted to be taken seriously as an actor. Brad knew it didn't mean he was about to be catapulted into the limelight. He still had plenty to learn, plenty of dues to pay. After all, he'd only been in California for six months, hardly any time at all.

The agent, though, had realized that Brad possessed a presence no amount of acting lessons could teach. Call it whatever you want—

attraction, charisma—heads turned to look at him. He smiled, and people remembered his face. It was only a matter of time before he'd begin to make his mark.

And that time was quick in coming.

A month later he auditioned for a part on *Dallas*. He made the callback, and then came the phone call saying that he had the role. It was nothing outstanding, just, as he called it, "an idiot boyfriend who gets caught in the hay" with Shalane McCall, who played the daughter of Priscilla Presley's character on the nighttime soap.

But it was a big deal to him, his first break. He'd achieved his goal—and with five months to spare.

With that, he felt ready to call his parents and tell them exactly what he'd been doing. His father's reply was simply, "Yeah, I thought so." Brad had to laugh. He hadn't been fooling them for a minute.

The work on *Dallas* wasn't too demanding. Mostly he had to look good—and younger than his twenty-three years—and smolder. He only had a few lines. But the character had been written in for several episodes, long enough for Brad's face to be noted and mentioned by the teen magazines.

In turn, Brad and Shalane noticed each other, and the two started dating. According to the *National Enquirer,* their relationship lasted a mere six weeks, although, "When Brad stopped dating her, she was devastated and cried for three days, telling friends, 'I loved Brad more than anything in the world!' "

He'd been fortunate to make his television debut on such a highly-rated series, even if it was in a small role. It looked good on his resume, and it also meant that a lot of the right people had seen him. They'd also been impressed, it seemed, because the acting work started to flow in.

From nighttime soaps he moved to daytime television, and a one-week stint on *Another World.* Again, it was hardly instant stardom, by any means, but it was solid work with a nice paycheck and a largely female audience that was ready to appreciate his good looks and build.

But when that was over, Brad was eager to stretch his limits. He wanted to act, not end up labeled as another TV hunk. So his agent began sending him out to audition for sitcoms. While he hated it, he was obviously doing something right, because he kept coming home with the parts. It wasn't constant employment, and all the parts were tiny, but it was work, putting his name and face in front of people, and it allowed him to pay his rent from his craft, which at the time meant real success to him. Finally it was real progress for an inexperienced actor. First of all there was *Growing Pains,* playing a not particularly nasty character, then *Head of the Class,* where he ended up staying for a few weeks.

Being on the set gave him a chance to meet one of the show's stars, actress Robin Givens. She'd been in the news on her own account recently, when her marriage to heavyweight boxing champion Mike Tyson disintegrated. A friendship quickly bloomed between Brad and Robin, then turned to something more, a relationship that ended up lasting six months.

It even managed to outlast a visit by a rather jealous Tyson. Brad was at Robin's house one night when the boxer arrived, not too pleased to find another man there. Luckily, it never came to violence, which was just as well; however muscular Brad was, he'd have been no match for the huge Tyson. Instead, the three talked, and the evening ended quietly. Not long after that, Brad and Robin stopped seeing each other.

Even in those days, Brad never had to pursue women. They simply came to him. He'd retained much of that Missouri shyness, an endearing quality in such a brash city. Added to his incredible looks, it made him a magnet. He was still very much a romantic, as he had been with Sara Hart in Springfield. He fell in love very easily, and liked to demonstrate his affection with presents—lavish ones that were often beyond his meager bank account. He'd go to his manager, Phil Lobel, asking for a loan to buy another gift.

Phil would shake his head and write a check. He knew Brad would soon be working again, that the loan would be repaid. And in a few months they'd be re-enacting the scene, as soon as Brad met someone new.

Brad continued to take acting classes with Roy London, and his efforts were really beginning to pay off. His natural charisma was really beginning to shine through on-screen, even in some dreadful roles. Directors noticed and remembered it, and the parts kept coming in. He landed a dramatic role on *21 Jump Street*, where, producer Philip Hasburgh told

People, "Brad walking into a room was more exciting than most actors doing a scene."

Then there was a brief spot on the highly regarded *thirtysomething,* under the direction of Edward Zwick and Marshall Herskovitz, who noted that, "He caused such a stir on the set. He was so good-looking and so charismatic and such a sweet guy, everybody knew he was going places."

Again, it was little more than a throwaway part, the boyfriend of a babysitter, but Brad made the most of it. What he didn't realize was that the impact he made there would come back to him six years later in much bigger ways.

Nineteen eighty-seven led to 1988, then 1989. Brad was working often, making ends meet, but not really going anywhere. He still hadn't progressed beyond minor characters, single "guest" shots or parts that lasted no more than a few episodes. Nothing regular or steady. It wasn't what he expected. You started at the bottom, then worked your way up. And at the moment, his elevator appeared to be stuck on the ground floor.

Then it began to move, at least a little. He auditioned for a movie, and got the part—not realizing he was taking the first step in a new, and eventually massive, career.

As a movie, *Cutting Class* was pretty bad. It was just one of any number of low-budget teenage slasher pictures coming out to exploit the success of movies like *Friday the 13th.* It was, as Brad later called it, simply "butt awful," the type of film that occasionally turns up late at night on some cable channel.

Even by the standards of the genre it was nothing special. It seemed to have been written and shot to a formula, not really aimed at theaters, but for the drive-in and video markets. Brad might have made it onto celluloid, but it was hardly something he wanted to crow about. And his movie debut wasn't exactly stunning, barely warranting a mention in the cast list. Still, he'd broken into a new field.

The film did do one other thing for his life—it gave him another new girlfriend. On the set he met Jill Schoelen, who was playing one of the leads, and it wasn't long before the two began dating. As usual, it wasn't a long romance, only three months, and ended before things became too serious. Brad was still searching for the right person, and he didn't find her in Jill. Not that he had too much time to go looking anymore, since his acting career had definitely moved up a gear. Between acting classes, auditions, callbacks, and learning lines, there was little enough opportunity for socializing, let alone romance. And Brad wasn't about to blow the chances that came his way; Bill and Jane Pitt had brought him up to be more responsible than that. But the work he was putting in was beginning to pay off. First he was in *The Image,* an HBO television movie. Then, finally, came his first big role, also for HBO, an episode of *Tales From the Crypt* entitled "King of the Road."

Brad starred as William H. "Billy" Drake, a heavily-tattooed, leather jacketed street drag racer, the best in Denver, who suddenly appeared to challenge a retired dragster known as "the Iceman," a man who'd buried his past—with its dark secret—and become respectable Police Officer Garrett.

Naturally, Garrett refused the challenge. But Billy proved irresistible to the Iceman's daughter (and it was here that Brad's looks and on-screen charisma made the character—a twisted James Dean type—believable in a story that was largely preposterous). Since Billy had no redeeming qualities, he kidnapped her, forcing the race.

Billy crashed and died, of course, justice seen to be done. It was, essentially, fairly mindless late-night entertainment with a brief homage to *Rebel Without A Cause* in the race scene. But Brad had shown he had the ability and presence to easily carry the weight of a story, and, even more importantly, that he could expand his range to convincingly portray a kind of edgy, controlled evil that would recur in a couple more roles later.

But that was the future. In the here and now, a first starring part was something worth celebrating. It was a major step forward, more exposure. And the more he was seen, the easier it became to get acting jobs. Nineteen eighty-nine had been the best year yet, by far. It really seemed as if he was on his way. He'd done remarkably well. In less than three years, with no previous acting experience, he'd garnered an impressive list of credits, and built a very solid foundation for a career, both as an actor and a face.

That impression was only strengthened when he auditioned for a second film, *Happy Together*, and ended up being cast. Again, the film was unexceptional, and Brad's part was minor, close to nonexistent. It was a college comedy, very mediocre fare, and, like *Cutting Class*, destined for the drive-ins and video stores.

However, it seemed to bring to light a problem that had been plaguing Brad throughout his short career. Yes, he was working fairly regularly, and in a profession where "resting" was a familiar part of life, he was grateful enough for that. But, at twenty-six, almost every character he'd played had been teen-aged. Even Billy had something of an adolescent air. Brad had taken to wearing an earring, but it didn't make him seem any older. To be fair, handsome as he was, Brad did look young for his age, young enough to believably play a high school or college student. Still, it was frustrating for him. He wanted more.

Things changed a little when he found himself picked for a type of work he'd never undertaken before—advertising. It was strictly because of his looks and build, but it was a quick shoot, the money was good, and he would finally be shown as a man—and a sex object.

It was for a product he was quite familiar with already—Levi's jeans. The main reason Brad had been chosen was that he looked so American, rugged, yet had a sensitive edge; the ad was for the European market, and the company wanted to project that all-American image.

As it turned out, the TV spot made quite a splash; not so much for Brad's bare-chested appearance, although that was noticed and drooled over by young women all over the continent, but for the music. It had become fairly common practice in Europe to use old songs in ads, and for this one the agency chose the Clash's "Should I Stay or Should I Go?" originally a hit in 1979, and which was now re-released, even though the band no longer existed, to shoot back up the charts.

If 1989 had seemed like a wonderful year for Brad, then 1990 was glorious. His reputation had grown. The momentum of his career had been picking up; now it seemed to be going flat out, and he was suddenly juggling all the work he could handle.

The biggest thrill was being cast in a television series. No guest roles or bit parts this time; he was to be one of the main characters in an ensemble, on *Glory Days*.

The Fox TV network was still in its infancy. It had just completed its first season. A few programs, like *The Simpsons, Married . . . With Children,* and *Beverly Hills, 90210* had done well, but others had quickly sunk. In an effort to draw in viewers, they decided to start the new season early—in July. After all, went the thinking, the competition was just showing re-runs. Offer people something new and they'll watch.

Glory Days was to be the centerpiece of Fox's new season. Six episodes had already been shot, and executives were confident of success. It was blue-collar, it was meant to be real, gritty, and quite human—the lives of four friends after high school.

So once more Brad would be portraying a teenager, but at least the character of Walker Lovejoy had some depth, something to get his teeth into. Lovejoy was still confused about life; full of ideals, he'd quit college in a huff after being kicked off the football team and was now making his way as a cub reporter.

It was a golden opportunity, and its failure had nothing to do with Brad, who, *People* noted in its review, "looks like William Dafoe's younger, cuter brother," acquitting himself perfectly well. There was certainly an irony in the former journalism major playing a reporter.

The premise definitely had possibilities. It

was, notably, a very male show, with no female leads, and with its emphasis on friendship and growth into adulthood. But, in spite of heavy advertising by Fox, it never caught on, and certainly wasn't helped by reviews that were, at best, lukewarm.

Variety described the series as "perfunctory" and Sam Weisman's direction as "without distinction," while David Hiltbrand, writing in *People*, thought "the dialogue all too often seems overwritten."

All six episodes that had been made were aired, but no more were ordered. Brad's chance of becoming a television star, a pinup along the lines of Luke Perry, faded abruptly. Maybe it was fate, he wondered, after getting the news. Maybe he could only ever hope for second best, supporting roles and bit parts.

In the end, it proved to be all for the best. There was no time for depression to set in. Before he knew it, Brad was offered two large parts, one in a film, the other in a TV movie. If the series had been picked up, he wouldn't have had the time to make them. And his career would have taken an altogether different path, ending who knew where.

Three

Brad knew it was impossible to turn down *Across the Tracks*. Never mind that he'd be playing a high-schooler yet again—and he swore this would be the last time—this role was simply too good. Opportunities like this didn't come often, and you had to grab them with both hands.

More than that, Brad knew he could relate quite easily to the character of Joe. A good, quiet son, an athlete—he'd been those things himself. He'd probably have to cut down on the cigarettes during filming, maybe even train a little bit, but he understood this part. And he was grateful for the chance to prove himself.

He realized it was still a B picture, that it wouldn't be packing them in for weeks at multiplexes around the country, but that didn't matter. This was more than a featured role, this was second billing. As soon as Brad went through the script again, he saw he had virtually as much screen time as the star.

Brad had kept his Missouri manners, but in other ways he was much older and wiser than the college kid who'd driven into town gawking four years earlier. It wasn't just that he'd grown up, it was the competition of the business, seeing friends give up hope and go home or find a more reliable kind of work. He'd even considered it himself a few times, in the early days when things looked particularly bleak. Go back, write that last paper, and get on with life as an advertising man. But not now.

Acting still didn't seem quite like a job to him. Yes, it was hard. There were long hours, take after take sometimes, but the unreality of it all was still fun. Watching himself become someone else, it was a thrill to him.

The idea of being a rock star hadn't entirely left his head, either. He still played, jamming with friends when he wasn't busy on the set. If somebody had offered him the chance to make a record, he'd have jumped at it. But he didn't have the time or the inclination to pursue it seriously. He already had his focus, and he needed to concentrate on that. Music was better as a distraction from reality, a dream.

He soon learned that *Across the Tracks* would star Rick Schroder, who'd come to prominence as a child actor in the movie *The Champ*, then gone on to star in the television series *Silver Spoons*. He'd been doing this kind of thing almost all his life, and Brad knew he could end up learning a lot from him.

The story was quite basic. The bad brother, Billy (Schroder), arrived home after a year in jail for car theft, genuinely intending to turn his life around. Joe, the good brother, the athlete, was working hard towards an athletic scholarship at Stanford. He resented Billy, whom he given up as an utterly lost cause. After a brief, sharp taste of his old life, Billy decided to keep to the straight and narrow. He began running with his brother—and discovered he had a natural gift. Joe, meanwhile, was tearing himself apart between school, work, and training. When Billy beat him at a track meet, he gave up—at least for one night, going out and getting drunk. In the morning Billy found him, the two talked, and with minutes to spare, Joe showed up at the county championship to run for his school. He beat Billy, who actually let him win, and got the scholarship.

At its heart, *Across the Tracks* was an "After-school Special" with earthier language. It was unabashedly sentimental, although it stopped short of being cloying. What the script needed to come alive was strong performances from the principals, Schroder, Brad, and Carrie Snodgress as their mother.

It wasn't a major motion picture. It wasn't even a potential hit. It didn't even have much of a budget. So, to keep costs down, it was set in California, near the water, handy for the studio.

Brad had run some track in high school, but that had been nearly eight years before. He began training, forcing himself around endless laps every day until he'd regained most of his old speed. If he was going to play a runner, then he'd be one. That was just the way he did things.

The filming was done in the summer. The production needed the use of a high school, and during vacation was the best time, since crew and cameras would be cluttering up the hallways. The great disadvantage to that was that the sun burned down on the actors as they shot the track scenes. After a couple of circuits in the heat, simulating a race, Brad felt like he'd been in the Olympics.

Not all the exhaustion was physical. With such a large role, Brad's talents were stretched in a way they'd never been before, and the skills he thought he'd developed as an actor were roughly tested. Under Roy London he'd really pushed himself, and now it all came to the crunch. Was he just the handsome face everybody saw, or did he have the ability to pull out the talent that might make him a star one day?

It turned out every bit as well as he could have hoped. Joe wasn't a particularly charismatic character—he was too good, too nice for that, really—but Brad made him memorable. More importantly, he made him believable.

Since Brad had been a well-behaved kid, a good boy, himself, there was plenty of his own adolescence he could put into the role. But there's a large gap between understanding and portrayal.

It helped that he was working with veteran talent. Rick Schroder bloomed in the part of Billy, overcoming the original tension between the brothers, then creating a new one as it became obvious that Billy was the better athlete. The two actors seemed to spark each other, as real brothers might, with love hidden under a lot of other emotions.

And, once more, Brad made a convincing high school senior, combining brash confidence in some things with an almost crippling shyness in others. Joe tried, but never fully managed, to hide most of his feelings by saying very little. But Brad made sure every single one showed on his face, letting the audience see what was really going on inside.

Across the Tracks was quite easily the best work he'd done so far. To a point it played on his looks, making him come across as cute and innocent, rather than handsome. Beyond that, it had all been up to him.

Joe desperately wanted the scholarship. Given that the family lived in a trailer, albeit a clean, bright one, it was obviously his only chance. The father, a drunken, demanding man who had expected his older son to excel, was dead, and the family existed from hand to mouth. Joe wanted to succeed, to be a winner. But he also wanted to shake off the ghost of his father, and not need to be the best at everything.

It was a subtle, internal conflict, difficult to put across without overacting or being maudlin. Yet Brad did fine, putting an edge on his goodness that let everything boil over occasionally. About the only scenes which didn't come seem quite credible were on his night of drunkeness, after he'd quit the track team.

But those were merely a set-up for the finish, the victory, and the final reconciliation between the brothers.

Across the Tracks had plenty of attractive qualities—Schroder's smoldering performance, Brad quite transparent as Joe, trying to stumble his way through late adolescence—but it was never more than a small film, which more or less guaranteed it instant obscurity. With no big stars, and a story that was heartwarming beneath its thinly gritty surface, it never stood a chance in the theaters. Indeed, most people never even had a chance to see it, and reviews were nonexistent.

It was a shame, really; the project deserved better. It offered some genuine insight into teenage lives, and showed the triumph of the straight and narrow path without ever becoming preachy. The scenes of athletic competition offered real drama.

While the movie slipped by unnoticed, it was still a good credit for Brad. Although he only merited second billing, he carried as much of the plot as Schroder; it was Joe's tale as much as Billy's. He carried it off effectively throughout. As an actor, Brad had developed to the point of being able to portray a full, rounded character, and given the chance to show that, he delivered.

He still had a roughness around the edges, but that was somehow part of the appeal, and made his performance seem more real and spontaneous. More than anything else, *Across the Tracks* helped define Brad Pitt as a real actor rather than just another face.

Not that he had anything to worry about there. If anything, he was becoming better looking with each year; the planes of his face were shaping into a rare handsomeness, and the camera was noticing. He was slowly developing the killer smile that could melt hearts and change minds. But in an industry where the extraordinary is the norm, he'd managed to show that he had more—much more—to offer.

Exactly how much became apparent in *Too Young to Die?* It was made for television, a movie of the week, but it gave Brad the opportunity to play the toughest character yet in his career. Billy was totally despicable, a coward, a pimp, and a drug addict. It was well beyond anything he'd done before, even Billy the drag racer. He wasn't even the center of the film—that was Juliette Lewis as Amanda Sue Bradley, her first starring role. But Brad's performance was so strong that it was Billy who stuck in the memory long after the titles had faded.

Shown on NBC, it was a fact-based story, questioning whether teens should be tried as adults and given the death penalty. Amanda Sue lived with her mother and stepfather in an Oklahoma trailer park. She was a good kid, nice but not smart. The stepfather abused her, the mother didn't care, and was just as glad when her sweetheart wanted to marry her, even though she was only fourteen.

The young marriage didn't last; neither was

ready for it. When it ended, Amanda Sue returned home, only to find that her family had gone, leaving no forwarding address.

With no money, no real education, and no prospects, Amanda Sue moved on to a bigger town, by an army base. In a bowling alley she met Billy, a good ol' boy who was really a loser, but hid it by talking big. He promised her a job, and got her one, as a dancer in a bar. Her life was sinking the way she'd expected.

Bad as he was, she clung to Billy; he was the only security she had. He fed her pills, used her for sex. At least, he did until she was spotted by a newly divorced army sergeant, who took her under his wing, and, for the first time in her life, treated her as a human being.

She quit her job and moved into his house, to look after his kids. It was meant to be a platonic arrangement, but eventually she found her way into his bed. She loved him, and she believed with all her heart that he loved her.

But happiness was never in the cards for Amanda Sue. Someone reported the sergeant for keeping an underage girl in his house, and he was given an ultimatum—get rid of the girl or be court-martialed. The army was his life.

There was only one thing he could do. . . .

Amanda Sue returned to the bar, and to Billy, who abused her, turned her out onto the streets as a prostitute, and introduced her to heroin. One night, high, the pair of them sneaked into the sergeant's house, and kidnapped him and his new girlfriend. Driving them out to the oilfields, Billy goaded Amanda Sue so much that she stabbed her former lover to death.

Although they ran, the pair was easily caught. Much of the drama centered around Amanda Sue's trial, the guilty verdict, and her eventual execution—the first minor ever to be sentenced to death.

And Billy? When the law caught up with him, he blamed Amanda Sue. She'd forced him into the murder, he insisted, he hadn't wanted anything to do with it.

The real tale, though, was in the circumstances that led up to the murder. Amanda Sue had been let down and abandoned by virtually everybody in her life—her parents, her husband, her lover. Even her only friend, a waitress she met, had moved away to marry. There was only Billy.

Juliette Lewis was exceptional as Amanda

Sue, overcoming a cardboard scripting of her character. There was so much more that could have been put in, horrific, true details of the girl's life, all edited out for the network, which disgusted Juliette. She was quick to point out, "The whole story was repulsive to me because it was cleaned up for TV."

Even Billy had been sanitized. But Brad had the ability to go beyond the written word and show the evil that was in the man. Portraying an Oklahoman was easy; Brad had known enough of them when he was growing up, even over the state line in Springfield. The accent was easy. But really bringing Billy to life was the greatest test of his talent.

A good deal of Brad's reputation had come from his looks, and now he went to great lengths to hide them. He wanted nothing about Billy to be obviously attractive. So he grew a thin, scruffy beard, and let his hair become longer and straggly, jamming an old baseball cap on his head.

Billy was down and out, living in his car, a parasite who readily cheated and used others to make his small way in the world. He existed in a single set of greasy clothes. Yet still, through him Brad radiated a rough power. He was as far from lovable, or even pleasant, as you could possibly get, but you couldn't take your eyes off him.

The past had shown that Brad was an improving actor, learning his craft and eagerly trying his limits. *Too Young to Die?* was his graduation. With this he was ready for anything. Roy London had done a superb job teaching him, and Brad had soaked it all up like a sponge.

His role as Billy was really his quantum leap out of the past and straight into the future. And he accomplished it mostly with small gestures. The smile still showed through, but instead of bright and sexy, he made it into a menacing leer. Waiting while Amanda Sue turned a trick, he conveyed both tension and resignation simply by the way he stood.

It certainly helped that there was a chemistry between Brad and Juliette, which became reflected in their screen characters. Billy had a faint tenderness for Mandy, even if he did use her. But Brad only allowed it to peek through when both the characters were high.

As an actor, Brad had become one for showing emotions on his face. He could communicate feelings without saying a word. It was a rare gift, and Billy was the perfect outlet for it—uneducated, a drifter, a man who could use words very persuasively but didn't know many. By letting the hard mask slip and the feelings slip out occasionally—even if they were mostly just anger or contempt—Brad was able to add a dimension that went beyond the writing, and make a full, rounded person out of the character on the page.

The challenge of doing that had obviously been one of the attractions in the role for Brad. In the script Billy was as two-dimensional as Amanda Sue, a stereotype of the good ol' boy gone bad. Adding the complexities and hinting at the depths was Brad's extra touch. But however much he made Billy seem rough and ready, there was obviously a great deal of thought and preparation behind Brad's performance. Instinct was a wonderful thing—and Brad's instincts always seemed to be on the mark—but hard work and research made the difference between good and outstanding.

One thing Brad quite obviously projected into the part was star quality; it was perhaps no coincidence that this would be his last television project before moving full tilt into a movie career. He'd come a long way from the callow young man who made his debut on *Dallas*. He'd developed the tools of his trade to the point where TV couldn't really contain him any longer; he needed a bigger medium.

Not that television doesn't use some great actors; it does. But simply by virtue of the budgets and schedule, it doesn't offer them the same opportunities as film, which is, quite literally, bigger than life.

With *Across the Tracks* Brad had enjoyed a taste of that, and he knew it was what he needed to fully develop his gifts. On the drive west from Missouri, he'd fantasized about one day becoming a movie star, but dreams were cheap and plentiful. The reality of his apprenticeship through bit parts and small roles was an experience that gave him a basis to work from. It wasn't so much ambition as a desire for excellence in his own work that carried him from there. Billy was the peak of his work so far, and it was as much as he could ever really achieve in television. Films remained the great challenge, and Brad was never one to shy from challenges.

Too Young to Die? had brought him to new horizons, more than he ever expected when he signed on for the job. Out of it came not only the desire to move completely into films, but something to fill another void in his life—a new girlfriend, Juliette Lewis.

Initially the two just worked together, developing their roles and exploring the relationship between their characters. It was purely platonic. After all, at sixteen Juliette was ten years younger than Brad, and, as he joked, the story didn't form the best background for love. "Yeah, it was quite romantic, shooting her full of drugs and stuff."

But it soon became apparent that there was something more going on. In *Rolling Stone* Juliette took up the story of how their relationship began.

"We got together to look at *Panic in Needle Park* for research, 'cause we had a shooting-up scene. So we hung out in this hotel room in Taft, outside of L.A., watching the movie. I noticed he had this black luggage, real organized. Matching. I have three different bags from all over. He had a CD case. I hadn't even moved up from tapes yet. He was, like, organized to a certain extent, and that was really appealing to me. He was just really authentic. So then we drove back together—two hours of good, quality driving. We didn't say much.

We listened to music. After that drive, we both knew we liked each other. We didn't even kiss. I was expecting it, because you move so fast these days. But he didn't; he gave me a hug. I tortured my best friend, Trish, over this for the next three weeks. Three weeks of, like, '*Oh my God*! What is he thinking?' "

Brad was thinking quite a few things. He liked her, every bit as much as she liked him, but there was a movie to shoot first. That was responsibility, work, and had to be taken care of before anything else. The chemistry between the two of them helped the filming, creating sparks that made Amanda Sue's return to Billy understandable, and even inevitable.

What Juliette had seen in Taft was the real Brad. He hadn't been trying to impress her; he was just his normal, everyday self, researching a character, listening to music, going about his life in a quiet, controlled way. Being organized was part of that. He'd developed an idea of the direction he wanted his career to take, and he was determined to make it happen.

Brad was used to girls coming on to him. It was something he couldn't control; it had been happening for a long time. Maybe he thought Juliette's infatuation was that, something that would pass in a little while. However, the more time they spent together, he realized that he was starting to miss her when she wasn't around.

"It wasn't until shooting ended that we both realized we wanted to spend more time together," Juliette continued. Away from the cameras, being Brad and Juliette with each other, rather than Billy and Amanda Sue, they knew it was love. This was the real, intense thing, deeper than anything Brad had experienced before, even back in Missouri with Sara Hart.

Juliette Lewis was still very young, but she was assured and mature for her age. The daughter of actor Geoffrey Lewis, she'd been bewitched by make-believe very early. By the time she was twelve she was working regularly in television, on sitcoms like *Home Fires, I Married Dora,* and *The Wonder Years.* Two years later, she petitioned the court to be legally emancipated from her parents. It had nothing to do with family relationships, which "couldn't be closer," but was a career move to free her from the restraints of child labor laws.

She moved away from the San Fernando Valley to Hollywood, where she roomed with a family friend, actress Karen Black, before renting an apartment with her best friend, Trish Merkens.

Brad and Juliette were soon an item around town, seen everywhere together, and very public with their happiness.

"She is truth!" Brad loudly declared about her, while Juliette told *People,* "He's like a painting. I wasn't looking for that. He just came that way."

As soon as the relationship was firmly established, they rented a small bungalow in Beechwood Canyon and moved in together. It was a major step—the first time either of them had made such a large commitment. But, as Juliette pointed out, they were "madly in love;" it felt like exactly the right thing to do.

Despite the age difference, in many ways they were a perfectly-matched couple. Both were obsessed with work, with being taken seriously as actors, and both were ready to move on to bigger things in their careers.

But many people thought it couldn't last, that one or other would get tired, that there'd be problems or ego or temperament. Brad was still the laid-back Missouri boy, meeting life as it came. Juliette, on the other hand, was intense, eager to experience everything, to run things.

Yet it worked. Love seemed to conquer all problems that came up.

They talked and worked out any problems that came up. Brad introduced her to music she'd never heard before. They discovered they both loved board games, and sat for hours in the evening playing Boggle or Mastermind. Juliette even began to cook for Brad, something she'd never done before.

"The womanly side of me just naturally comes out with Brad," she explained. "I mean, imagine me cooking? But I finally learned how to steam rice for Brad. I made rice and steamed vegetables and chicken dogs from the health food store for a week straight. Every night. At first he was like, 'Oh God, that's so sweet.' Then he was totally like, 'Hon, couldn't you learn to make something else?' "

Really, there were like any other young couple, in love and learning to be together, wrapped up in each other. The relationship gave them both a center to their lives that had been missing. For Brad, certainly, the idea of family and home was deeply ingrained; it was something he'd been searching for but hadn't found in any of his previous girlfriends. The two of them began to talk about getting married, and making plans for the future.

No sooner had they begun discussing that, though, when everything had to be shelved. Work called. For Juliette, it was a part in Martin Scorsese's remake of *Cape Fear,* which would begin her rapid climb to stardom. For Brad, the role was in Ridley Scott's new movie, *Thelma & Louise.*

He'd never expected to get it. He knew he wasn't the first choice; that was William Baldwin. But Baldwin backed out, having been offered a larger slice of screen time in *Backdraft,* and Brad got the call. Without hesitation, he went and read with Geena Davis.

"It just sparked," he said. And that was it—he was in.

What he didn't know was just how much it would change his life.

Four

Thelma & Louise found its place in the American consciousness through controversy. It was big news. Debates raged in the press, in cafes, bars, and offices around the country as to whether it was a feminist movie or just entertainment, a buddy movie like *Butch Cassidy and the Sundance Kid,* only starring women.

But underlying it all was another, darker factor. This was a film about girls with guns, who weren't afraid to use them. To a lot of people, particularly men, that seemed threatening.

Not to Brad, though.

"I don't think the movie has some big moral the way a lot of people are making out," he said in the *New York Times* when it was released, "and I don't find it controversial." He would, however, concede that it was a slap in the face "for us guys—and we deserve it."

The discussions about the film were publicity that no amount of money could buy, a drawing card far bigger than any of its stars. Audiences kept coming to see it, then talking about it, which drew in more people, and the circle just grew.

Whichever angle you took on it, *Thelma & Louise* was definitely one of *the* films of 1991. At its heart it was really about female bonding, about friendship and the sacrifices and forgiveness of friends. What made it interesting was the story it told, and the way it told it.

The women were, naturally, the center of attention, and no one would deny that both Geena Davis and Susan Sarandon were excellent in the title roles. But their vibrancy was highlighted by making most of the men in the film very dowdy, and often stereotyped, from the clichés they spoke, to their clothes, and even the way they were lit.

The only character to escape that was Brad's

J. D. Although he was a thief, he had some life about him, some color and personality. He was most certainly the only man to leave any real impression after the house lights had come up.

It was a small part, really, not much more than a few minutes on-screen. And to a large extent Brad's performance was ignored by the critics, who saw J. D. as just another twist in the story, or, perhaps, another example of men using women. So why, then, did it prove to be such an important turning point in Brad's movie career?

To the jaded reviewers he might not have seemed anything special, but to thousands of women who spent their money to see the film, Brad was something else. Rarely had such a small amount of screen time had so much impact. Yes, he was a thief, he stole the money that would have seen Thelma and Louise safely to Mexico, but the audiences were more than willing to overlook that. A fair number of them might well have thought it was worth $6,700 to enjoy the night Thelma did with him. Without a doubt, it was one of the most sensuous, sexy love scenes in a major motion picture. Which made it all the more ironic, according to a crew member, that Brad's "biggest concern was that his mother wouldn't approve." The Missouri boy obviously hadn't gone too Hollywood.

Filmed from Texan Callie Khouri's script, the film was the story of waitress Louise (Susan Sarandon) and housewife Thelma, played by Geena Davis, who plan to take a weekend vacation together, just the two of them, away from their menfolk. But, like all the best-laid plans, it was destined to go awry from the beginning.

Thelma's husband, Darryl, a successful salesman who also happened to be an utter jerk, put his foot down. So Thelma left him a note about where she was going attached to a frozen dinner in the microwave, and hopped into Louise's convertible with her luggage and a gun, for protection.

Setting off on a beautiful Arkansas day, it all seemed perfect. Thelma was feeling frisky, having briefly broken away from the only man she'd ever known. The trouble began when she persuaded Louise to stop at a bar. Getting drunk, and approached by a stranger, Thelma accepted an offer to dance. But her friendliness was misinterpreted. He hustled her outside, and attempted to rape her.

It was broken up by Louise, who pulled Thelma's gun on him. It was all over, without a shot, until he insulted her. She pulled the trigger, and he was dead.

The pair realized they had to run—who would believe their story? Louise, it was hinted, had been in similar trouble before, in Texas. Where could they go? Louise's answer was Mexico.

Stopping to call Louise's boyfriend, Jimmy, a sympathetic musician who'd always been afraid of making a commitment to her, they headed south. He was supposed to wire money; instead, he was waiting for them.

But along the way, Thelma had insisted they pick up a hitchhiker, J. D., a polite, handsome young man who did incredible things to a pair of jeans, and who claimed he was on his way back to college.

Jimmy had brought the money, all $6,700 of it, enough for Thelma and Louise to make their getaway and start a new life. Louise left it in the motel room with Thelma while she went to talk things through with Jimmy.

What she hadn't banked on was the return

of J. D., seeking a little shelter from the storm, which turned into a night of sex and Thelma's first-ever orgasm. J. D. charmingly confessed that he was, in fact, a robber, and gave Thelma two lessons in the art; the first when she demonstrated how he conducted his business, the second when he vanished with the cash.

By now all manner of police were onto them, camping out at Darryl's house and tapping his phone. A state investigator tried to persuade them to turn themselves in. Louise turned him down flat.

They were on the run, and they had to move fast. Heading south, out of money, Thelma tried what J. D. had taught her, and held up a small country store. They were getting in deeper all the time.

But they were also freer, more careworn and desperate, but living a life that was far removed from the ruts they'd dug themselves into, making their way across the deserts of New Mexico towards the border.

Encountering a truly disgusting truck driver, they lured him off the highway, then used their guns to blow up his rig. It was a gesture of empowerment, that they could live life on their own terms. But the authorities were closing in, the chances were getting fewer. They'd gone from freedom to fugitives.

Evading police cars, they took off into the mountains, thinking, perhaps, that they'd escaped, that they could make it. But as the view behind them opened up, there was a seemingly endless line of vehicles, lights flashing in pursuit.

Finally, they were cornered. There were two options—forward, over a cliff to certain death, or back, to surrender, prison, and a lifetime of the confinement of which they'd finally broken free. For Thelma and Louise, the choice was remarkably simple. They hit the gas pedal and flew.

It was one of those few movies that succeeded in being thought-provoking while it entertained. No one left the theater without an opinion. The script cleverly raised questions that it didn't try to definitively answer. Ridley Scott's direction stirred the visual senses. From the moment the first reviews appeared, it became the cause celebre of 1991.

To be sure, there were plentiful echoes of road movies and buddy movies, like *Butch Cassidy and the Sundance Kid* or *Easy Rider*, both of which had serious moments mixed in with their banter. But at the same time, *Thelma & Louise* contained faint shades of crime-spree films like *Badlands* and *Sugarland Express*.

None of those, though, had ever centered around women. The idea of women taking their future into their own hands was something completely new for Hollywood, and, to a large extent, for America. According to the magazine *America*, what was put across was "a highly ambiguous message. Freedom is exhilarating, but it is also destructive," making it "two movies in one." *The Christian Century* announced firmly that it was "not a feminist diatribe but a female buddy–road movie," a view also taken by Britain's *New Statesman*, which defined it even further, as "a 1970s buddy road movie."

Rolling Stone, while accepting that it was a "road movie," also pointed out that "Khouri's script isn't about rage or revenge; it's about waste," and described the film as "wincingly funny, pertinent and heartbreaking . . . get[s] under your skin."

The New Yorker didn't take it quite as seriously, saying that it had "a pleasantly dreamy quality," and summing up, "In the end,

Thelma & Louise seems less a feminist parable than an airy, lyrical joke about a couple of women who go off in search of a little personal space and discover that they have to keep going and going and going to find a space that's big enough."

If even the critics were unable to agree about the movie, offering as many opinions as there were writers, what was the public to think?

That was perhaps the beauty of it—everyone could place their own interpretation on it without ever being wrong. Soon it wasn't just movie reviewers who were writing about *Thelma & Louise*, but editorial journalists as well. The controversy even made the cover of *Time* as people expressed their views.

It had achieved the rare status of moving beyond cinema to invade everyday life. There were even bumper stickers for people to display—THELMA AND LOUISE WERE RIGHT—jokes and cartoons. Every little bit helped make it more successful.

From the outset it had been obvious that it would have some impact, but no one would have dared predict what did happen. Brad couldn't have picked a better vehicle for his major film debut if he'd tried. Backing out from the part of J. D. was the greatest favor Billy Baldwin could have done for him.

Not that the role alone made him. It was what he did with it. Underneath it all, J. D. was a fairly unsavory character—a real charmer, but also a robber, a thief, a con man, and a seducer. They were hardly the qualities to bring out anyone's sympathy. What Brad did was take those attributes and stand them on their heads to make J. D. seem a rogue rather than an out-and-out criminal, and a sweet, sexy rogue at that. How did he do it?

"Ridley [Scott, the director] would let us play around a lot," he explained. "He'd say, 'Okay, we got that one, now let's try something else.' "

Much of the movie came out of these improvisations. So, in other words, J. D. was as much Brad's creation as anybody's. But that was perhaps fair. Brad knew those Oklahoma boys all too well. He'd grown up around them and their kin. He might well have known someone just like J. D., back in Missouri. He certainly had no trouble with the accent and the southern politeness. He'd never robbed anyone himself, but in many ways J. D. was as close as he'd ever come to playing himself, all the way to the down-home charm and the smile. Billy, in *Too Young to Die?* had been from the same area, but he was too dark a character to ever to make Brad a star.

Still, said Brad later, "I figured it would be a role like J. D.—something I'm good at, a Southern guy—that would make the break." And, he added, "It basically opened the door for some kind of respect, working with all those great people."

Sure, Brad had been working fairly regularly before, certainly more than many in the acting profession. But soap operas, sitcoms, and slasher movies were still the lower end of it all. There wasn't much chance for an actor to show his skill. However well he'd performed in *Across the Tracks,* few people were ever likely to know, simply because it wasn't a big feature. His face, and to a lesser extent, his name, was known, but that was about it. He'd needed a real break into the movies.

Thelma & Louise was his perfect vehicle for the change. Being in a film with people like Susan Sarandon, Geena Davis, and Harvey Keitel was the kind of opportunity that didn't happen every day to someone like Brad. It was his big shot and he had to make the most of it. And he did.

"People are either stars or they're not," film director Neil Jordan said. "They either project or they don't. The minute Brad walked into *Thelma & Louise* he did that. He was a star from then on."

That was a bit of an exaggeration; Brad still had some way to go before he was a real, acknowledged star. But there was absolutely no doubt that the movie sowed the seeds of his huge fame. He entered the set an unknown, and emerged as someone much bigger. He had the type of charisma, the presence, that hadn't been seen for a long time. When the camera focused on him, you had to watch; there was simply no choice.

Of course, what most people remembered about Brad in the movie was his hot sex scene with Geena Davis, "one of the rare sex scenes that manage to be funny and truly erotic at the same time," as one reviewer stated. "There's one glamorized shot of Brad Pitt's torso that suggests a commercial for sex, but at least the image expresses Thelma's gaga emotional state at that moment." It was true; the image that branded itself on peoples' minds was of

Brad above Geena on the bed, his washboard stomach looking like a promotion for *Abs of Steel*, before the two of them crashed riotously and joyously onto the floor.

While there were plenty of women in the audience who would gladly have traded places with Geena Davis and her "$6,000 orgasm," as Brad called it, what came across as steamy on film was really quite clinical on the set.

"He was absolutely charming, very shy and nervous," was the recollection of one technician.

Brad himself said later "I mean, how seriously can you take it?"

Thanks to Ridley Scott's direction, plenty of people were able to take it very seriously. To audiences, he became almost as big a part of the movie as Thelma and Louise themselves. Perhaps it was because he was the only male character who had any sort of sexuality about him that wasn't completely disgusting or degrading to women. He used Thelma, but in return he gave her the best night she'd ever know. To some extent, it was an even trade.

Almost overnight, the movie transformed Brad Pitt into an American heartthrob, a film pinup. Amazingly, there was no hype, no publicity machine working to make that happen. It came from the people who paid to see the movie. Although he protested, "I don't go around robbing people, and I wouldn't say I'm that great in bed," nobody wanted to be convinced, especially when the rumors began that he'd had an affair with Geena Davis during the filming. Whether it was true or not didn't matter; it sounded good. Besides, she'd just broken up with her husband, Jeff Goldblum. Who could blame her for finding that body irresistible?

But there was really far more to J. D. than a roll in the hay. After all, he was the one who gave Thelma her lesson in armed robbery. Hair dryer in hand, white Stetson on his head, fine physique on prominent display, he demonstrated that it was quite possible to be gentlemanly even while committing a crime. While it was overshadowed by the sex, this was really the better scene, where Brad was able to draw the most from his portrayal. The cocky slant of the hat, the slightly awkward cowboy formality of the language, and above all, the wide, white smile, combined for something quite magical.

J. D. stole the motel scene, although the other side of his character appeared a little later, under questioning from Harvey Keitel's Arkansas state investigator. The politeness was still there, but it was a veneer for cowardice. It was a scene that Brad played more with his face than with his words, admitting gradually that he'd stolen the money. Then, on his way to the cells, protected by guards, he could afford to taunt Thelma's husband, knowing he was safe from any physical assault.

Those scenes are not quite so well remembered. Perhaps it was because the thrust of the story had moved on, to the point where J. D. was largely irrelevant. Or perhaps it was because there was no joy in them. They were the "typically" masculine side of the film, full of threats and sexual bragging. In the motel J. D. had been something slightly larger than life, a young stud almost out of a dream who could transport Thelma. Even his crime seemed relatively minor in comparison. Under police questioning the image crumbled to leave someone very ordinary. It filled out the character, but most people seemed to prefer the memory that stayed with Thelma, among them the critics, who tended to notice the body and the charm, but forgot the rest.

Rolling Stone called J. D. "a hitchhiking hunk charmingly played by Brad Pitt," while *The New Yorker* pointed out that the character was played by "Brad Pitt, who has the sullen handsomeness—and the white cowboy hat—of the country singer Dwight Yoakam."

It certainly helped that the photography, editing, and direction were all excellent. Ridley Scott had a very powerful visual sense, honed by a background making commercials, before moving on to features like *Alien, Blade Runner, Black Rain,* and *The Duellists.* As *The New Republic* commented, "he again shows how he can make the modern world—this time the American Southwest—deliver up visual treasures." To *America,* "He creates a visual world as seen through the eyes of two women who have become exhausted with their small-town Arkansas lives." Others weren't quite so kind, finding his attention to detail somewhat overwhelming: "Scott still seems to thinks that 'Interior. Morning' in a screenplay translates as 'special effect.' "

Still, he did a great service to Brad, showing him in a far more flattering light than he'd ever enjoyed before, and winning him the instant admiration of thousands upon thousands of women. More than that, by making him a hunk, Scott changed Brad Pitt into a known Hollywood name.

And if being a hunk was the way he could enter this new world of bigger movies, well, Brad certainly wasn't about to turn it down. Heartthrobs might have been "a dime a dozen," but the plain truth was that he had all the qualifications—the perfect manners, the glorious face, and the body. As he realized, "only you know what you got in you," and once he'd entered this charmed circle, he could do what he'd been doing all along, and prove himself as an actor.

The only problem was that the scripts which started arriving in his mailbox all called for him to play variations on J. D., something he wasn't about to do. Once was fine, but, as had always been the case with Brad, having done it, it was time to move on. He had no wish to be typecast as anything.

However, until the movie actually premiered, he had no idea just how great the impact of J. D. was. As Juliette Lewis recalled, "I went to Brad's premiere for *Thelma & Louise*. Everyone was screaming: 'Brad! Brad! Over here!' The flashbulbs are exploding in your face. It's like a brainwashing trip. You could be brainwashed into being forever dispersed and just lost!"

It was a shock. He knew he'd done good work, the best of his career, and he knew he'd certainly made the most of his big opportunity, but he'd never expected such an overwhelming response. The teen magazines had found him when he was on *Dallas*, at the beginning of his career, but that attention had quickly faded, and Brad imagined that no one outside the business or his family really knew or cared who he was. But these people did.

To his credit, Brad never let himself get caught up in the fuss that ended up surrounding his appearance in the movie. It had opened the door for him, but he didn't need—and didn't want—to be seen as some new sex symbol who'd fade away in a few months. He was realistic—and self-deprecating—enough to see it for what it was, just a nine days' wonder. And he was comfortable enough with himself, and his relationship with Juliette, not to need the adulation.

His refusal to capitalize on J. D. did have a down side, however. A few months later, when Brad had already moved on to other projects, he attended the premiere of Juliette's movie, *Cape Fear,* the vehicle that made a star out of her. It was her bright moment, and he was keeping to the side. Suddenly a light turned on him, and a voice came, wanting to ask him a few questions. Out of politeness, Brad obliged.

"How does it feel to be on *Beverly Hills, 90210*? began the voice. All Brad could do was laugh.

"I'm not on *90210,*" he replied. As quickly as it had appeared, the light vanished.

"I mean, just like that," he said in astonishment. "Fade to black. I got a kick out of that."

How quickly they'd forgotten. But one thing was certain, they'd soon be remembering again.

The success of *Cape Fear* made the relationship between Brad and Juliette equal again. His sudden popularity was matched by hers and they became L.A.'s young hit couple. Not that they were about to let themselves start believing that.

"He's from Missouri," she said of Brad in *New York* magazine. "He's not at all an L.A. stud–type person."

But they were both hot properties in Hollywood. It was an unreal time for them both, feted, wined, and dined when they simply wanted to be at home listening to music, playing board games, or going out with friends. Brad might have been a wonderful body onscreen, Juliette might have come to shocking prominence for the scene where Robert DeNiro stuck his thumb in her mouth, but they were *actors*.

Juliette summed up what they both felt when she told *People* magazine, "I've been working for years for this. Success is a nice byproduct, but what I really want is work."

And work was coming—all they could handle. Juliette had already agreed to act in a new Woody Allen movie, which was a lengthy time commitment. Brad was in the midst of his next three pictures, roles so different from J. D. that he hoped he'd be more or less unrecognizable. And he already had big plans for the future.

What he really wanted was for the two of them to move away from the non-stop hustle of Los Angeles. Not too far, just northern California, still readily accessible for Hollywood, but removed and private.

He also hoped to be able to secure financing for a project that had been simmering inside him, a film about the doomed jazz trumpeter and vocalist Chet Baker, who'd been something of a heartthrob himself in the 1950s. The idea was that Ralph Bakshi (with whom Brad was working on *Cool World*) would direct, while Brad would take the starring role.

"I want to play Chet Baker because I love his music and because I'm fascinated by characters like him," Brad said. "People who have so much, yet somehow just can't get it together are very mysterious and compelling to me."

It was a dream, and, like most dreams, destined never to see the light of day. But it said something about the roles that were closest to Brad's heart, the romantics whose fates were dark, however much they might try and kick against them. With characters like Johnny Suede and Tristan in *Legends of the Fall,* he'd come back to this type of person again and again, identifying in them the romantic heart that beat in himself. Even Louis, in *Interview with the Vampire,* had some of these qualities, although time had long since hidden them. But in Brad's portrayal they managed to peek through.

The move to northern California was another dream that never happened. Brad and Juliette stayed in Los Angeles. At least, it remained their home base. Most of the time their house stood empty while they were away on location shoots, with only their brief moments of being together before the next film began. It was a hard life, but neither would have had it any other way.

Five

Well before *Thelma & Louise* reached the theaters, Brad was back to work. The word was already out on his riveting performance, and people in the industry were starting to look closely at him. Scripts were piling up on the table, waiting to be read. But in the meantime he'd contracted to appear in *The Favor.*

It was a change of pace for him, a way of showing a different facet of his acting ability. He'd done the television sitcom apprenticeship, and *Happy Together* had been vaguely funny, but neither had really shown *his* comic side. *The Favor* looked as if it might.

In the end, it didn't. In truth, the movie

didn't show much of anything, something quickly realized by the executives at Orion, who let it languish on the shelf, unreleased, until 1994, when it finally appeared, not on screen, but on video. Even that, it might well be suspected, was only because Brad was in it. His name was becoming bigger by the day, and the company saw a way of recouping some of its investment.

Brad played Elliott Fowler, an up-and-coming twentysomething Portland artist, and the younger lover of a successful gallery owner (Elizabeth McGovern). Initially it seemed as if Brad's main job in the film was to show his good looks and torso as much as possible, but things rapidly became more complex.

The plot centered around a housewife's recurring fantasy of seducing the high school boyfriend she'd never slept with. Tied into a happy but humdrum marriage with two children, Harley Jane Kozak's character was plagued by dreams of what might have been. So when McGovern went to Denver (where the old boyfriend now lived), she was persuaded to look him up. And, improbably, sleep with him—the favor of the title.

She did, and returned, ecstatic about her

night of sex. However, that was where the problems began. Soon she discovered she was pregnant, unsure whether the father was her friend's old beau or Pitt, whom she'd recently dropped.

As in any dutiful comedy of errors, the situation became more tangled, with suspected affairs, recriminations, and finally a climax in Denver, where all the characters gathered. The old boyfriend was shown to be a complete idiot, McGovern realized that she loved Brad after all, Kozak's marriage was neatly patched up, and everyone lived happily ever after.

It was fairly mindless entertainment, not exactly a high point for any of the talent involved, but at the same time it wasn't a total embarrassment. If not for the somewhat adult nature of the situation, it would have been perfectly passable television fare.

At least *New York* magazine enjoyed it, finding it unusual for a movie to feature "a normal grown-up"—in this case McGovern's character—noting that, "Unfortunately, the phenomenon has become as rare in our infantile movies as the appearance of a Martian in Central Park."

On the other hand, *People* couldn't summon up a single scrap of enthusiasm for the project, pointing out that "*The Favor* cannot lay claim to a single plot twist that is at all new or interestingly redone," and closing, "The cast members, particularly [Bill] Pullman [who played Kozak's long-suffering husband] and Pitt, deserve an audience's deepest, deepest sympathy."

The two opinions were about as far apart as it was possible to be. But *People* was certainly right in highlighting Brad's performance in what was otherwise a fairly routine exercise. Along with Elizabeth McGovern, he stood out, and not just for his face or physique.

As in *Thelma & Louise,* his looks were just attractive starting points. The character of Elliott Fowler contained surprising depth. He was successful, but still confused about what he wanted in his life. He was willing to make an emotional commitment, yet scared of it. Above all he was a genuinely nice guy, trying hard to do the right thing. The only problem was, he hadn't completely figured out what the right thing was.

Portraying the flip flops of such a personality wasn't an easy job, particularly when the script dealt with them so tritely. However, Brad was more than up to the challenge it offered, and once again he was helped by the fact that his face could reflect so much of what was going on inside, be it turmoil, joy, or sadness. Luminous, he transformed what was really a secondary character, a stereotyped cipher, into a real human being.

Indeed, part of the growing reputation he was enjoying as an actor was that he could communicate so much with very little dialogue. As a natural gift, something that could never be fully taught, it gave him an edge, and enabled him to really explore his roles and offer a fully rounded realization in his portrayals, something he'd come to use more and more in the parts he'd take.

Brad and Elizabeth McGovern were able to generate a believable chemistry that extended beyond the bedroom to genuine caring, again giving the movie a depth beyond the written word. In that regard it was far more than what *People* wrote off as a "giddy romp, which compares unfavorably with a *Love, American Style* segment," but overall, it was certainly not what it could have been, and that wasn't the fault of the cast. They all gave rock-solid performances.

Brad was brought into this project as the resident hunk, but by the time it was over, he'd managed to surprise quite a number of people with his talents. He more than lived up to the buzz that was beginning to circulate and that would become all too clear on the release of *Thelma & Louise*; he was going places, and he'd be reaching them very quickly.

As it was, he'd already signed on for his first starring role, although it was hardly for the big-budget fare he'd soon be making. Instead, it was for a quirky, offbeat little film that would very likely gather no more than a cult audience, if that. As an unexpected move, this was one of the best. But *Johnny Suede* wasn't a movie that Brad made to advance his career. His already knew that his future lay with major motion pictures where he would be seen by millions of people. This was an art picture, one he worked in purely to satisfy himself.

Its big appeal to him—apart from being completely over the top—was the fact that Johnny was a musician, a man who desperately wanted to be a rock 'n' roll star, and Brad, of course, had never lost his love of music. There was still a little part of him that wanted to be up on stage with a guitar. But deep inside he understood that this role would probably be as close to it as he'd ever get.

It was fun. It was bizarre, completely out of

left field, and it was decidedly hip.

Johnny's greatest features were his massive pompadour, his black suede shoes (which had magically fallen from the sky one day), and an overwhelming desire to be a teen idol just like his hero, Rick Nelson. His private world was the neo-fifties, in the way he dressed, sang, and lived.

The movie more or less chronicled his on-again, off-again relationship with Darlette, played by Alison Moir, who finally tired of Johnny's obsessions and his failure, causing her to return to her old lover, successful photographer Flip Doubt, even though he was in the habit of beating her.

After losing her, Johnny met another woman while on his way to band practice. Yvonne, a teacher, was the most—actually the only—faintly realistic character in the piece, grounded with a proper job, a fully furnished apartment, and a connection to life.

It seemed unlikely, but the two fell for each other, and after weighing the pros and cons, Johnny moved in with her. But he missed his freedom, and the feeling that domesticity was taking away his chance in the music business kept gnawing at him. Finally, after an argument, he left, only to eventually return, realizing that he loved her, and that their love was more important than anything else.

As a story it was very thin, but it was never meant to be a strongly plotted film, more a series of vignettes to put across an idea.

For the very first time the weight of the movie rested completely on Brad's shoulders. He was in every scene, he was the focal point. It was a huge responsibility, and, as if that weren't enough, he had to pull it off while playing a character of almost childlike innocence.

For under the rock 'n' roll bravado, Johnny Suede was a dreamer, sensitive and tongue-tied, confused by the world and afraid of it. He believed in magic, and in music, but it was a long time before he could come to believe in anything as real as love.

Those were the challenges and contradictions Brad faced in the part.

"I want to keep the work interesting," he'd said when he signed to make the movie, and this certainly gave him every opportunity to do just that.

In so many ways he was the ideal choice for Johnny. Much of what he communicated had to be done subtly, without language, and Brad had already proved he was more than capable of that. But now he was able to take it further.

Part of it came from James Dean, in the sullen, almost childish attitude that Brad showed when Johnny didn't get his way. The rest Brad invented. For the *New York Times*, he "flashe[d] some of the characteristics of the young Jack Nicholson," although his performance really seemed less mannered than that. Reviewer Vincent Canby did temper that slightly harsh judgement, though, by pointing out that he seemed to be "a genuine movie personality." The simple fact was, Brad actually managed to make Johnny believable, bewildered flesh and blood rather than the cartoon he could so easily have been, particularly with the outlandish hairstyle (as it was, Brad had to endure two to three hours each day getting the wig right before filming could commence).

It was no small achievement, and he did it the way he'd brought his other characters to life, through the small gestures and the openness of his face. Johnny needed subtlety to work, and Brad had it, which prompted *Rolling Stone* to praise his "memorably offbeat performance," while *Variety* felt he "[gave] Johnny the right kind of innocent appeal."

There was also plenty of fun for Brad—who was a major heartthrob now that *Thelma & Louise* was had arrived in theaters—in playing a would-be idol, someone who failed where he seemed to be effortlessly succeeding. It gave him a chance to laugh, not just at the process, but also, a little bit, at himself.

But when casting for the film began, his name was nowhere near as well known, to the point where writer/director Tom DiCillo had a tough job persuading his producers to accept Brad. They wanted someone familiar, someone who would bring in the curious, and Brad Pitt was hardly a household name.

DiCillo stuck to his guns, though; he knew Brad had exactly the qualities he needed for Johnny.

Of course, once the first footage was seen, everyone knew DiCillo had made the right decision; Brad *was* Johnny. He was perfectly natural, creating sympathy for someone who, in the wrong hands, would have come across as just stupid.

Off-camera, Brad was the perfect southern gentleman, winning female hearts all over the set with his looks and gentle behavior.

"He's so good-looking, intelligent and sen-

Brad in an early publicity shot.
(John Paschal/© *Celebrity Photo*)

Picture-perfect.
(John Paschal/© *Celebrity Photo*)

Visible in this shot from the early days is Pitt's resemblance to another screen heartthrob—Robert Redford. (Ron Davis/*Shooting Star International*)

With Shalane McCall,
who played his girlfriend on "Dallas."
(© *C. Delmas-Sygma*)

Relaxing in Los Angeles.
(© *C. Delmas-Sygma*)

Out on the town with *Married with Children*'s Christina Applegate.
(John Paschal/© *Celebrity Photo*)

With his parents, Jane and Bill Pitt, at the premiere of *Thelma and Louise*.
(Gamma-Liaison © *Barry King*)

With ex-longtime love Juliette Lewis at the Academy Awards. (Gamma-Liaison © *Barry King*)

With Tina Louise, his co-star in *Johnny Suede*.
(Porva/© *Sipa-Press*)

Brad with Dennis Hopper outside Mann's Chinese Theater at the premiere of *True Romance*.
(Vincent Zuffante/*Star File*)

Camera-shy with Robin Givens.
(Vincent Zuffante/*Star File*)

Brad steps out with current girlfriend Gwyneth Paltrow, who he met and romanced on the set of *Seven*, in which she played his wife. (© *Rex USA Ltd.*)

At the U.S. premiere of *Interview with the Vampire*.
(*AP/Wide World Photos*)

At the premiere of *Interview with the Vampire*: with co-star Tom Cruise...

...and the cast of *Interview* (*left to right*: Stephen Rea, Christian Slater, Cruise, Kirsten Dunst, and Antonio Banderas). (Both photos © *Berliner/Liaison USA*)

Pitt being presented to Prince Charles at the London premiere of *Legends of the Fall*.
(© *Rex USA Ltd.*)

sitive," said Tina Louise, the biggest star in the cast (she had played Ginger on *Gilligan's Island*), while a technician on the set noted that he showed none of the phoniness or emptiness that sometimes accompanied fame.

"He was pretty real, very low key. He even went out with the crew a few times while we were filming. Not a lot of actors do that."

But to Brad, the crew was just as important as he was. They were all part of a team, professionals and human beings who deserved to be treated politely, and with dignity. That was the way Bill and Jane Pitt had raised him, and he knew it was right.

His friendliness towards everyone extended beyond the time of filming. Brad remembered the people he worked with. When *Johnny Suede*'s costume designer, Jessica Haston, died of a brain tumor two years later, Brad flew to New York to attend her memorial service. It wasn't something he *had* to do. They'd enjoyed no relationship beyond work. He'd become a star, a bit name. No one had ever expected him to be there. But, without any fanfare, he flew across the country to pay his respects. It was, in his world, just what you did.

* * *

As everyone had expected, *Johnny Suede* did well on the festival circuit. At Locarno, in Switzerland, it was voted Best Film, winning the Golden Leopard award. It proved incredibly popular at Robert Redford's Sundance Festival, before going on to further festival success in Toronto and Deauville. The praise was unanimous: *Variety* called it "easily likable" and "a new contender on New York's cult film scene," while *Rolling Stone* deemed it a "stylish debut" for director DiCillo.

That was enough for it to be released to mainstream theaters, although not widely. With Brad's stock rapidly rising after his performance as J. D., it was thought that his name would help draw people in, then word of mouth would help generate wider circulation.

Unfortunately, that never happened. The movie died. Brad might have been hot, but even he couldn't generate enough of a flame to get bodies in seats for this. It was too esoteric, too strange, for mass consumption. Brad might have looked good, and given a superb performance, but *Johnny Suede* simply wasn't the stuff of movie hits even if, as *Playboy* said, it "reaffirms Brad Pitt as a screen legend in the making." As it was, after a couple of very slow weeks in the multiplexes, it moved to the art houses, where business was somewhat better.

But even there, it never quite clicked, never made it to cult status, which could have kept it playing forever on the midnight circuit, like *The Rocky Horror Picture Show.* So it vanished, only to return a few months later on video.

Brad was disappointed, but not too surprised. He hadn't expected much beyond enjoyment when he undertook the project, and he'd had his share of that. Besides, he was already in the middle of an extremely demanding new project, *Cool World.*

It was the inspiration of Ralph Bakshi, the man who'd made a small name for himself in the seventies with the adult animation feature, *Fritz the Cat.* This was to be something different, a mix of live action and animation, which, he planned, would take the technical tricks of *Who Framed Roger Rabbit?* one step further.

It was a movie that *all* the Hollywood faces wanted to be in. Brad was up against some two hundred other actors—many with much bigger names than his—for the role of humanoid policeman Frank Harris.

"Brad walked in the room," Bakshi recalled, "did a reading, and blew me away. I thought he was the only one who could do this part."

But, just like Tom DiCillo, Bakshi had a tough time convincing the producers that he was exactly the right person for the part. They wanted a top star; he held out for Brad.

In the end, Bakshi won, and Brad was cast along with Gabriel Byrne and Kim Basinger. Now the pressure started. Brad was in, and he had to perform.

It was utterly unlike anything he'd done before. For most of the filming, Brad was working in a vacuum, alone on a soundstage, trying to interact with invisible characters, the cartoons—or doodles, in the language of *Cool World*—that would be drawn in later.

Certainly, he was stretched as he'd never been before, to make something so unlikely seem possible, talking to the air, surrounded by technicians. Indeed, Brad said that it was impossible to have an ego, trying to act alone to an audience of technicians.

Virtually everything, right down to the love scenes and fights, were done that way, with no one to give him a reaction to bounce off.

"It just became a dance," he commented later.

Which was all it could be, at the time.

The finished spectacle was anything but

empty. Cool World was an incredibly full place, jammed with the history of animation, its clichés and possibilities. And Brad's Frank Harris was the 'noid cop who had to look after it all.

Transported there after a post–World War II motorcycle accident which killed his mother, the prime directive Harris had to maintain was no sex between doodles and humans—those few who came through. That created problems between him and his doodle girlfriend, Lonette, but Harris was a man of principle, a true forties noir detective, tough on the outside, but with a soft, caring heart underneath.

Jack Deems (Gabriel Byrne) was a cartoonist, an ex-con who thought he'd created Cool World. And to humans, at least, he had, making a fortune off the comic books he drew about the place. Freakishly, though, he suddenly found himself shuttling between real life and what he thought was his imagination, in the process meeting Kim Basinger's character, Holli Would, the sexiest doodle ever, whose driving ambition was to become human. And she knew exactly how to achieve it—sleep with a real person.

With Holli as a seductress, Jack never stood a chance, even though Harris tried to keep him on the straight and narrow. It happened, and Holli took on the flesh and blood form of Kim Basinger. Jack and Holli returned to the real world, trailed by Harris, for a final showdown in Las Vegas.

Trying to prevent Holli from reaching the "spike of power," Harris was killed, and Holli opened the space between the two worlds, flooding Earth with doodles. But Jack, a good man who didn't understand the implications of his actions, proved to be the eventual hero, making up for his mistake, and returning things to their rightful state.

Holli was back in Cool World, a frustrated cartoon again. Jack remained in Vegas. The only outstanding question was, what about Frank Harris? In perfect cartoon fashion, his death was only temporary. The only difference was that he was reborn as a doodle, much to Lonette's (and his) delight. And so everything turned out just fine in the end.

Cool World should have been a smash. It had all the elements—groundbreaking use of new technology, excellent performances, and an attitude that was hip without being overwhelming. Instead it flopped right on its face. With everything going for it, how could that have happened?

The answer lay in *Variety*'s review of the movie, "an ordeal . . . in the form of trial by animation. . . . Bakshi has let his imagination run wild with almost brutal vigor, resulting in a guerrilla-like sensual assault unchecked by any traditional rules of storytelling."

It was, really, *too* busy. Almost every second had two or three things going on; at first it was merely distracting, then after a while it became wearying. As a display of the cartoonist's art, *Cool World* was masterful. Unfortunately, to tell this particular tale, it was just too much, or, as the *New York Times* put it, "Mr. Bakshi's skill as an animator continues to outshine his judgment about subject matter."

The reviews barely mentioned the human actors, which, in the rush of color and action that overwhelmed them, probably wasn't too surprising. Although they were supposed to carry the story, they ended up taking the back seat.

Byrne, Basinger, and Brad were all superb. Brad in particular seemed to work with the doodles as if they'd been on the set with him throughout the shoot.

There was no doubt that Bakshi made the

right decision in hiring him. Very few other actors had the ability to emote so well without words, to react so much.

And he looked great. The forties style of baggy suits and slicked-back hair suited him, although, in truth, there seemed to be no way he could appear bad these days. And here, given a Bogart-style role, he was in his element. Of the human performances in *Cool World*—even compared to Basinger's smoldering Holli—his was by far the most memorable.

By now he'd proved beyond any doubt that he could invest even the shallowest of characters with a range of emotions, and give them depth. He was certainly the only person who didn't look completely lost in this film, who seemed to have a real grasp of what he was doing, and why. It was even easy to believe that he was happy to stay in Cool World, rather than ever go home, because home was where pain was. In a single statement he was able to put across many shades of feelings, from fear to hurt, and even resignation.

All along in his career, he'd been pushing himself, showing all the things he could do.

"I have to find something I can do and go out and get it," he told journalist Chris

Mundy. "Then they go, 'Oh, he can do that.' But wait, there's more. I want to do *this* now."

Having filmed three movies back to back, Brad had covered a lot of ground in a very short time.

However, working so much, often away from home, had kept Brad and Juliette apart. Not that she hadn't been busy herself, filming *Cape Fear*, then Woody Allen's *Husbands and Wives*. But, as she said, "What's not easy is the separation. . . . The hard thing is keeping good communication when you're three thousand miles apart."

Still, the relationship remained rock solid. They relished what little time they were able to spend together, staying at home, rather than club-hopping and being targets for the paparazzi.

"All that young Hollywood indulgence . . . and excessiveness is just sort of boring," Juliette said. She much preferred "getting caught up on my relationships."

Not that she had to worry about Brad while he was away. He had the looks and charm and sex appeal, but she knew he was faithful to her.

"He's the most naturally monogamous creature I've ever run into, male or female," she said with certainty.

Everything was on very firm ground between them. Having that sense of stability at home—even if his girlfriend was every bit as busy as he was—helped him. It gave him a center, a sense of happiness that he truly appreciated. Underneath the actor and his increasingly laid-back way of looking at life, was a southern boy who cherished family.

Brad had accomplished a lot in the last couple of years. He'd moved up to a higher league. J. D. had done an awful lot for him, and he knew it.

The only problem was that since then he'd been involved with three flops. That would have sent a lot of actors into tailspins of panic, but Brad barely stopped to think about it. He'd been working, the movies had been interesting and challenging, and that was his main concern. There'd be plenty of other good opportunities coming down the pike.

And there were. They were coming his way all the time. The studio executives knew a true star in the making when they saw one. The choice of roles was largely his, and he agonized over it. He wanted parts with some resonance, that would keep stretching him. He was going to be doing this for the rest of his life, and he was determined to make a mark of some kind. So he read through scripts for art films, strange films, and, finally, more major films. Among them was one he just knew he couldn't turn down.

Robert Redford had optioned Norman Maclean's autobiographical novella *A River Runs Through It* a number of years earlier, and commissioned a script. Now he was ready to film it, and he asked Brad to test for the part of Paul, the bright but doomed younger brother of the family.

It was an interesting choice. Again, it was totally different from any other character Brad had portrayed. Bright, outgoing, and physical, Paul had plenty of dark, hidden depths. He was the golden boy who was tarnished underneath—the kind of character a younger Redford could have played to perfection.

Brad jumped at the chance to do it. After *Cool World* it would be a pleasure to work with people again. And, with Redford's participation as director and plenty of studio money, it would be a good production, one that wouldn't get lost within a couple of weeks of opening.

Six

At first glance, a movie whose main activity was fly fishing in the wild rivers of Montana would seem to be unlikely commercial Hollywood fare. However, Robert Redford saw a great deal of merit in the story of two brothers, Norman and Paul Maclean, and he had the name and the power in the industry to make the films he wanted.

He already had been successful as a director with *Ordinary People* and *The Milagro Beanfield War*. But in this, Redford, a dedicated conservationist, had the opportunity to show the Montana waters—beauty of nature unspoilt by man—that had become defiled as the century progressed; it was as much mission as work for him.

People seemed to either love or hate Maclean's autobiographical novella. In the *New York Times,* Caryn James called the book "sugary enough to make your teeth ache," while in the *Wall Street Journal* Julie Salamon found it to be "an enchanted piece of writing."

Redford was all too aware of the contradictions. He knew that the essence of the story was "maddeningly elusive," and made sure that the script took great pains to strike a delicate balance, leaving it, as Salamon said, with "enough poignancy and beauty."

In light of the rest of the casting, it wasn't so surprising that Redford picked Brad to play Paul. Neither Craig Sheffer, who would play Norman, nor Tom Skerritt, chosen to portray the father, was particularly well known to movie audiences. Only Emily Lloyd as Jessie, Norman's girlfriend, had any real movie name, and even that was minor. This was a film about characters and relationships rather than big stars.

Of course, Redford had to be aware of Brad. The fuss that had surrounded *Thelma & Louise* had finally died down, but an impact had been made. In his connection with the Sundance Film Festival, he certainly would have seen an advance screening of *Johnny Suede.*

Paul was the golden boy of the Maclean family, the one who'd broken out of the mold to live life on his own terms, rather than conform to society's aspirations. He was charming, a talented newspaperman, and above all, a naturally gifted fly fisherman. He had glamour. But he also had his dark side, the one that would eventually cause his downfall. He drank to excess and he was an unsuccessful gambler, constantly in debt.

To bring Paul to life, a charismatic actor was needed, one who could show effortlessly the range of the man's qualities. Brad was the obvious choice. In the story emotions were rarely discussed; the Macleans weren't a family that discussed their feelings. So they had to be put across in other ways. Brad, of course, had that enviable ability to show emotion in his face, without the need for words.

For his part, he was ecstatic to be involved with the production. Redford had a reputation for making quality films that really tried to say something. It would be another major release, which would put Brad back in front of a large audience. Finally, the role of Paul looked to be a real challenge, not least because Brad would have to learn the art of fly-fishing—and appear very convincing doing it, too.

The script had some changes to the story for the sake of drama, but kept all the major incidents. At heart it was the story of two brothers, Norman and Paul Maclean, sons of a Scottish Presbyterian minister, growing up in Montana in the early part of the twentieth century.

The Reverend Maclean had two passions—his church and fly-fishing, the latter of which he passed on to his sons, particularly Paul.

Growing up, the boys had their wild times—stealing a boat and riding it over the rapids for a dare—but Norman grew out of that. He traveled east to attend Dartmouth College. Paul, however, chose to stay in Montana to become a reporter on a small-town paper, a undemanding job that left him plenty of time for fishing, as well as drinking, womanizing, gambling, and fighting. The wildness never left him.

When Norman returned, the differences between the brothers were obvious. Norman was the sober, industrious one, ready to tread the straight and narrow, while Paul, the golden boy who could have been successful at almost anything, had let himself get further and further out of control.

Only in fishing could he ever find peace. The brothers fished together often on the Big Blackfoot or another river, wading into the water and enjoying the challenge of catching trout. Their father had taught them a lot about the sport, and both had learned well. But Paul had gone far beyond that. His talent, it seemed, was God-given.

Norman continued to live with his parents; Paul had his own place. Norman began to date Jessie, a local girl; Paul caroused with Indian women. He began to grow deeper in debt to an ongoing poker game he was certain he could eventually win.

On a fairly regular basis Norman would receive calls in the middle of the night, and have to drive to town to pull Paul out of the jail cells where he'd been put after drinking and fighting. Paul was going downhill fast.

Finally Norman was offered the job he'd hoped for, teaching at a university in Chicago.

He asked Jessie to marry him; she accepted. He'd be leaving, again. For one last time, the brothers took their father fishing.

Both Norman and Reverend Maclean had a good day, but this outing was Paul's time; he could produce magic with the rod. They watched as Paul hooked a fish and played it, finally following it underwater, downstream, tossing and tumbling through the rapids, until it finally gave up and he reeled it in.

But the joy couldn't last. Shortly after that day, just before Norman's departure, another late night call came in. This time Paul wasn't in custody. He'd been found in an alley, beaten to death. All the bones in his right hand—his casting hand—had been broken.

The plot line was fairly slim. More than anything, this was a film of textures and moods. Paul was the heart of the story, always present even when he wasn't physically on-screen. But there was a mystery about him, something never quite knowable, a depth that couldn't be plumbed.

It would have been all too easy to fall into the trap of becoming sappy and maudlin, which, thankfully, the movie avoided, as

Caryn James was quick to point out in the *New York Times*: Redford had created "an unsentimental film about a past that is ripe for cheap nostalgia. . . . Anyone who expects this film to be simple-minded and simple-hearted is coming from the wrong direction."

It would also have been remarkably easy to have made a boring film. Fly-fishing, after all, was never meant as a spectator sport. Instead Reford made it into a joyous celebration, more an affirmation of life than anything else.

With Paul, Brad had a heavy load to carry. In *Johnny Suede* and, to a lesser extent, *Across the Tracks* he'd been the center of a movie. But neither of those had been widely seen. To most people this was his first starring role. Paul was also a far more complex character than Johnny; putting across the full range of his personality required a great deal of subtlety, things left unsaid as much as spoken. Brad knew there was going to be a lot of pressure on him in this one.

Even before filming began, there was plenty for him to do. At home he began to practise casting with a rod, spending several weeks standing on the roofs of buildings in Hollywood—the only places around where he could work on the technique he'd been taught. As he quickly realized, it was very much an acquired skill, and for a while he found himself with the hook ending up in the back of his head. Once it even had to be dug out with pliers.

By the time he left for filming in Montana, though, he'd managed to master the basics, enough, at least, not to embarrass himself. Then, up in Big Sky Country, there were more lessons, both in fishing and the local accent. Only then was he finally ready for the role.

He made plenty of friends on the set, often among the locals who had been drafted in as extras. But for the most part, he was content to spend his free time alone, exploring the area with the coon hound he'd adopted, or just sitting and reading in his small, rented apartment.

Redford handled the voice-overs of an older Norman remembering the past. Not that he needed to make an appearance in the film; given the way Brad looked, anyone would have thought he was a young Redford from the *Butch Cassidy* time. With bright, shiny blond hair and a mischievous grin plastered across his mouth, Brad's resemblance to Redford was uncanny. But, the *New York Times* commented, "The resemblance probably has less to do with the director's ego than with Mr. Pitt's charismatic presence and ability to project Paul's glamorous aura so powerfully."

For the film to work Brad had to deliver a charming, captivating performance. That was exactly what he managed to do. This wasn't Brad the body. This was Brad the actor truly stretching himself to fill a very demanding role, and showing that he had everything it took to be a major star.

It certainly helped that, as producer Patrick Markey said, "The camera loves him."

In *Thelma & Louise* it had been evident that he was the focus of attention during all his scenes. All eyes simply were drawn to him. Here, competing against the wild backdrop of Montana's natural beauty, he did it again, not just for a few minutes, but over the entire course of the movie. He *was* the compelling young man Norman Maclean had seen in his brother.

Mostly Brad's performance and the charisma he was able to bring to it were responsible for his successful transformation into Paul. But, to be fair, a few little tricks were used to heighten the contrasting personalities of the brothers. Paul was supposed to be "golden," so he was the blond in a family of brunettes. The dark, sober colors of the house typified most of the Macleans, who were shown always slightly in shadow. Paul, though, was lit differently. Outside, the sunlight caught him. Inside he always seemed to be sitting in the perfect position.

The character of Paul gave Brad his chance to consolidate the impression he'd made as J. D., and there was no chance he was going to blow it. This time the reviewers had no choice but to take notice of him.

"In Paul's tones of voice," wrote one critic, "and the expression of his eyes, often seen in close-up, can be read, like reflections on shifting water, the tiniest fleeting presences of jealousy giving way to generosity over Norman's good fortune . . . until, for one shattering instant outside the gambling hall, Paul's eyes give away the desperation that will destroy him."

It wasn't a personality formed through speeches—Paul wasn't one for talking a lot—but through a number of subtle gestures, building up an overall impression. But, for all that one critic thought he'd succeeded remarkably well, David Ansen, writing in *Newsweek,* wrote that "Brad Pitt has glamour and charisma, but he can't show the demons pulling this golden boy apart."

Those were typical of the reactions, however. People either found Brad completely believable in the role or hated him. There wasn't, it seemed, any middle ground.

To Julie Salamon, "Brad Pitt . . . looks a little like the young Robert Redford and has the charm to make us see Paul the way Norman saw him." But for the *National Review,* "Brad Pitt, his hair dyed blond, makes Paul a heady charmer indeed, doubtless not coincidentally looking just like a young Robert Redford; there may even be some real acting buried under all that charm." *New York* magazine phrased it a little more pithily: "Playing this extravagant ideal, pretty Brad Pitt doesn't so much act as throw himself into and out of rooms and flash his candy smile. He may be a good actor, but one can't be sure."

Interestingly, not one of the reviewers questioned the way Brad looked as a fisherman. He'd learned quickly, and well, to the point where he appeared totally at home up to his waist in a chilly, rushing Montana river with a fly rod in his hands, as if he'd spent his entire life doing it. Those were, understandably, meant to be the scenes with the most life and joy about them, lovingly captured like old memories.

Overall, *A River Runs Through It* was an ambitious film, and one that Redford obviously made for personal satisfaction rather than with any expectation of huge box-office success. It was "a film whose subtlety and grace disguise the fact that this is an artistically risky project." That was true. But obviously it worked, since, in the final analysis, the same writer found it "beautiful and deeply felt." John Simon, in the *National Review*, was far less kind, dismissing it up as a project that "tells you everything about fly-fishing that you never would have dreamed of asking," and full of "homespun sentimentality . . . in inexhaustible supply." The *New Republic* failed to find "the connection between the action of the story and its aura." The magazine did conceded that "Redford couldn't have directed more reverently," but it concluded "the very act of filming makes this an incompleat angler." David Denby hated Brad's performance, and wasn't convinced by the movie as a whole, but did allow that "in the fishing scenes . . . Redford achieves a sense of wonder that is quite satisfying."

Redford himself was "satisfied" with the way the film turned out. It was impossible to capture all the nuances of Maclean's work, or his portrayal of a family that couldn't communicate its emotions. Paul had always been the center, but where the novella looked at him plainly but kindly, the movie put him on a pedestal and made him larger than life.

There were very few actors who could have been convincing in the role. It demanded a special combination of screen charisma, good looks, and physical presence. At the same time, the person couldn't be too well known, too associated with other parts.

So Brad was the only real choice. In playing Paul, he truly fulfilled the potential he'd shown in *Thelma & Louise*. But where that film only gave him a few minutes, here he had almost two hours to demonstrate the full range of his talents. And they were plentiful.

Over the course of the previous two years Brad had truly honed his skill. By picking projects that challenged him, he'd grown as an actor to the point where he'd become one of the leading lights of a generation that included names like River Phoenix, Christian Slater, Keanu Reeves, Tom Cruise, and Johnny Depp. If he wasn't quite as well known as the others, it was just because he'd spent his time portraying characters rather than trying to play himself.

Brad stood well apart from the rest of that crowd. He wasn't a Hollywood socialite, a club hopper. Once the flurry of publicity that surrounded *Thelma & Louise* had died down, the paparazzi had ignored him. Which suited him perfectly—he was more interested in improving his craft than in having his picture pasted all over the gossip columns.

A River Runs Through It was the culmination of what he'd learned. He *became* Paul Maclean, and Paul became him. His performance, under Redford's direction, was completely natural and convincing. Of course, there was much he could relate to in Paul. Brad himself was someone who tended towards few words, and wasn't quick to talk about himself. But, in the most important respect, they diverged. Brad might have enjoyed his beer and cigarettes, but he didn't have the self-destructive impulses that kept Paul running throughout his life.

The movie garnered mixed reviews from the critics, but in the public's judgment it was a hit. Redford had a reputation for being a little bit of a maverick in the industry, making films that stood just outside the standard commercial mainstream, but films that were possessed of real quality. Initially, that was what brought people out to the theaters. But once they were won over—and it wasn't difficult—the word passed and the film did great business.

It was the most satisfying kind of success to have. People were surprised to discover that fishing wasn't boring, and, in fact, that it could be exciting. When Paul emerged from the river, soaked to the skin holding a large fish, the audience shared the triumph in his wide grin.

Then, when the voice-over flatly related his death, audiences felt a real sense of loss. Paul had been so full of life, it seemed impossible for his end to have been so sudden, and so sordid, even though all the signs had been in place. That was the beauty of what Brad had created in the role, someone bigger than life, who lived on after the movie as if he'd been a part of the viewer's family.

For all that, though, Brad wasn't pleased with his work. He'd been under a lot of pressure to deliver a powerful performance. In his own estimation his work had been weak, which led him to say, "It's so weird that it ended up being the one I got the most attention for."

But, as he told *Movieline,* he also felt that "there's no getting around it. Redford did a fantastic job crafting that film, shaping it into chiseled granite. A film adapted from a book's got to take its own form—Redford did that."

Certainly it didn't hurt the movie's impact that it was filmed during a glorious Montana summer, with its sheer, wild beauty forming a constant backdrop to the action. Or that, by setting it in an era far enough removed from today's problems but with enough of today's conveniences, it cast a rosy glow of nostalgia without seeming like history.

Brad summed it up: "It's an afternoon movie. Can't go see it in a big crowd. You gotta see it in the warmth of the afternoon."

Certainly the lingering impression was hot

sun on water and the cool shade of trees. But, as Redford intended, the face that stuck in the mind was Brad's. *Thelma & Louise* had brought him to public attention. It had made his reputation as a face and a body, and made a minor star of him. *A River Runs Through It* transformed him into a real star, an heir to Redford in his own way. He was handsome, overflowing with charm, full of the screen charisma that could capture a generation, and an actor of seemingly unlimited potential.

While Brad insisted, "I don't want people to think I'm the next anything," Juliette Lewis was saying, "I'd like nothing more than for him to become the next Robert Redford. If he started getting mobbed whenever we go out, sure, that would be annoying. It already is. But he's not turned on by anonymous pretty bodies. They're just bodies."

Even more than before, the future was wide open for Brad. Once again his name was on everybody's lips. He could have had his pick of parts. No one would have blamed him if he'd chosen something very visible and glamorous to make his breakthrough complete. After all, he'd spent six years paying his dues and working his way up the ladder.

But he'd already rejected the easy route once, after *Thelma & Louise*. Handsome faces and hard bodies were ten a penny in Hollywood. What he wanted—and what he needed, for his own satisfaction—was to be taken seriously as an actor. Everyone seemed willing to concede that he had charisma, and that the camera loved him. Perhaps because of that, words about his ability were fewer.

"All of a sudden . . . people are telling you you're worth this, you're worth that," Brad had explained. "You're worth more than you feel, and what they're really telling you is that now you have something to lose. And so actors start operating out of fear . . . emphasizing all these other elements that have nothing to do with the art."

The art of acting fascinated him. *That* was important, not the business. He was making money, getting prime, juicy, interesting roles, and he wanted to keep it that way, not be swept up into that tide of image and power and fear. He was also tired of being separated from Juliette. Since moving in together both their careers had taken off. When they finally were able to manage a few days at home together, they were exhausted.

The solution to both Brad's problems came in a screenplay forwarded by his agent. The movie would give Brad the chance to make an abrupt U-turn from the character of Paul. Also, since the studio was strongly interested in having the two of them together, it would give Brad and Juliette the opportunity to work together again.

It was simply too good to pass up.

"I asked for it," Brad later said. "I picked the hardest ones I could find. And, damned right, they were."

That was precisely his interest. It would be difficult, a constant challenge. Being a heartthrob was going to happen—it had happened already, really—it was out of his control. Being the best actor he could possibly be *was* in his power, and he was determined to make it happen.

It wasn't the characters with the sharp, witty lines that attracted him, he explained. "I'd rather see people dealing with problems, trying to get around them. There's places for both kinds of roles, but what I respect is this thing of seeing people trying."

He knew he couldn't be outstanding in everything; Brad didn't try to fool himself into believing he was the greatest actor ever. Some things would work exceptionally well, others would be best forgotten. But without trying, without pushing the limits, he'd never really know what he could do. As he'd realized after *Thelma & Louise,* it was all just a game, and it was always up to you to show what you really had inside.

He was still in the process of finding out exactly what he had in him. Bill and Jane Pitt had instilled in all their children the idea that if a job was worth doing, it was worth doing well. The job Brad had chosen was acting, and he wasn't about to start coasting now.

So *Kalifornia* was perfect. There was nothing "cool" about the character of Early Grayce, no pithy one-liners to enhance his reputation. Quite the opposite. As a sociopathic hillbilly serial killer, Brad would be back to playing a villain, but this time one with no redeeming features. Juliette would play his girlfriend, Adele Corners. Simple, tolerant of the abuse heaped upon her, she was a variant on Amanda Sue Bradley, and something of a forerunner of the character Juliette would play in *Natural Born Killers*—an area she seemed to be staking out as her private preserve.

For both Brad and Juliette, the idea of working together seemed wonderful. After all, they'd met that way, and things had flourished. Now they really knew each other, and they'd become better actors; they should be able to give great performances. More than anything, it would mean an end to that separation, at least for a while.

The pundits looked on Brad's decision doubtfully. He seemed intent on throwing away a potentially great career to prove something that didn't really matter anyway. People didn't care how well or how badly you could act. It was the way you looked up on the big screen that mattered. What they couldn't understand was the pride Brad took in his craft. Having discovered his talent, he wanted to take it as far as he could. If that meant being less commercial, well, that was the path he'd follow. But business definitely wasn't going to be his emphasis. Maybe he'd never get rich, but he'd be able to face himself in the mirror every day.

So the papers were signed, and Brad and Juliette began their preparations for *Kalifornia*.

Seven

Juliette was already skinny, but the role of Adele required her to look like a rail, someone with a malnourished childhood, who looked gawky and awkward in any type of adult clothing.

For Brad it was exactly the opposite. Early was the type of man who existed on fast, cheap food and beer. There was still muscle on his body, but most of it had gone to flab and fat. It was what the character needed, so Brad added twenty pounds to his frame and practiced the stoop-shouldered walk so often seen in the South. This also had the effect of making him seem smaller, compressed, always ready to strike.

That was a good start, but it wasn't enough. Brad didn't want any trace of the hunk in Early, so he let his hair and beard grow, rarely washing them, until they were lank and greasy; he soon looked far more like a bum than any kind of movie idol. It was about as far from a pretty boy image as he could possibly travel.

"I wanted to do one of those trailer-dwelling, greasy nails guys—no education, canned food, real white trash. . . . It's the farthest thing from Golden Boy."

The producers were ecstatic that Brad and Juliette had agreed to do the movie. They were both well-known young names, perhaps not as familiar as some, but with established followings and powerful credentials. The script was strong. Everything looked set for a big movie.

Early and Adele were the center of the film, but its momentum came from the two supporting characters, Brian Kessler (David Duchovny, who would go on to find his own success in television's *The X-Files*) and his girlfriend, Carrie Laughlin, played by Michele Forbes.

Kalifornia was really a dance among the four of them, although Brad chose to describe it as "a musical quartet."

Early was the lowest of the low. He lived with Adele, his waitress girlfriend, in a trailer parked in a Pittsburgh junkyard. On probation, he had no job, a sullen, edgy attitude, and a quick temper; he was pure "trailer trash." He was behind on his rent and his probation officer was giving him a rough time. The audience's first view of him said a lot—throwing a large rock off an overpass in the rain to cause a car wreck, then walking away to the diner where Adele worked to eat chili.

Brian and Carrie, on the other hand, were a pair of arty yuppies. He was fascinated by murder, and wanted to write about it. She found her thrills in photographing erotica. Their home was a carefully decorated loft, their orbit one of gallery openings and drunken parties.

The two worlds collided when Brain decided to make a tour of historical American murder sites as research for a book. He could write about them, Carrie could photograph them. They'd finish in California, the place she wanted to go, since she had begun to feel stifled by eastern galleries who kept rejecting her work.

Brain advertised on the bulletin board of a local college for riders to share the gas and driving. Sent there on a job interview by his probation officer, Early saw the notice, and realized it was an ideal way for he and Adele to get out.

On the morning the trip was to begin, Early and Adele were waiting as Brian and Carrie drove up in their vintage Cadillac convertible. The pairs were a deliberate study in contrasts—the yuppies in stylish black, hair and clothes perfect, while Early wore an old baseball cap, T-shirt, and frayed work pants, and Adele attempted to look nice in an outdated, hand-me-down frock.

What Brian didn't realize, as he pontificated about theories of murder while he drove, was that he had a real-life murderer in the back seat: before leaving, Early had killed and robbed his landlord, then set fire to the trailer.

The four headed south to Tennessee, the first of Brian's murder sites. But, as he talked to the owner of the house, failing to be invited in, Early walked around to the kitchen window and stole a purse.

That night, in a motel, Carrie expressed her reservations about Adele and Early, but Brian cast them aside. They'd made their commitment, they had to go on. And so they did.

The traveling continued, winding across the south towards Texas. In the evening Early took Brian to a roadhouse, a bar populated by a strange—and unlikely—mix of white and black, rockers and rednecks, all large and drinking heavily. It was no shock that someone tried to pick a fight with Brian as he played pool. The surprise came from Early, who exploded a hail of blows and kicks, completely demolishing the man.

That was the start of an odd bond between Brian and Early. Brian saw something in the hillbilly he lacked, a macho quality he wanted—at least for a while.

In a gas station Early followed a man into the rest room, and quite casually knifed him to death before robbing him, then used the money to pay for the gas Brian had just pumped.

It was a situation rapidly running out of control. The problem was that Brian and Carrie had no idea of the depth of it. Carrie still wanted to dump Early and Adele, but by now Brian was having absolutely none of that. He liked Early; after all, the man had saved him from a beating.

Then the man taught him to shoot at an abandoned warehouse in Texas. To his astonishment, Brian liked it. Carrie, of course, didn't. She saw the way Brian was changing, coming under Early's spell.

It was inevitable that things would collapse sooner or later. The time came at a small gas station, where both Carrie and Early saw a news item about Early being wanted for murder.

That was the turning point. Until then Brian and Carrie had held some faint power over things. Now that control passed to Early. He shot the attendant, bundled Carrie back into the Cadillac, and had Brian drive.

They went as planned to the next murder site, an old mine in Nevada. Early's plan to kill his witnesses was hampered by the arrival of the state police, who had no idea what they had driven into. Without even thinking about it, Early shot them both, then sneered at Brian when he wouldn't finish them off.

The road trip of discovery had turned into the road trip from hell. Even the mousy Adele, who truly loved her man although though she had suspected what he was really like, was terrified.

Taking over a house in the desert belonging to an old couple, Early killed the husband and threatened to kill Brian, who he saw as just another weak individual. Adele tried to keep things human, but it had gone well past that. Early had gone past everything. Pistol-whipping Brian, he took off with Carrie; when Adele tried to stop them, he unblinkingly shot her.

Regaining consciousness, Brian followed them. The Cadillac's radiator had exploded in a ghost town—part of a nuclear test site on the Nevada-California border—and it was here that Brian caught up to them.

Early was the expert in violence, but Brian had been his pupil, the one who'd learned quickly and who had the desperate edge this time. Even so, it seemed an unfair contest. Early was faster, heavier, and by this time, quite psychotic.

In the pitched physical battle it was give and take, until finally Brian seemed to kill Early.

He then released Carrie. But it wasn't over yet. Like any evil being, Early just refused to lie down and die. This time it seemed that Brian was going to lose, until Carrie fired the gun she picked up off the floor—and fired and fired. It was over.

Carrie and Brian stayed together, in California, finding a house on the ocean and some measure of peace. Brian had photographs of Early and Adele, tapes of them talking, and his own memories of the journey, but, in the end, he couldn't bring himself to write about it. It was too close to home.

The movie should have been a success. It had all the right elements—Brad and Juliette, suspense, lovely photography. But it ended up not doing particularly well, despite a heavy advertising campaign.

The problem was that it was too dark. America had long had a fascination with killers of all kinds, as long as they offered some kind of mystery or glamour. Early Grayce had neither. Not too long after *Kalifornia,* Oliver Stone would release *Natural Born Killers,* also about serial killers but with a much more glamorous sheen, and it would go on to become one of the hits of the year, both in terms of money and sensation.

Kalifornia wasn't helped by being largely ignored by reviewers. That was a shame, because they, and the public, missed an exceptionally good movie.

At first glance, all four of the main characters were little more than caricatures—the trailer trash and the yuppies. But as the story progressed through its twists and turns, the actors were able to invest each of them with individuality.

Brad and Juliette in particular were superb. Juliette's Adele was a woman-girl, naive, but with a strong sense of understanding and compassion. She could even forgive Early when he beat her, because, she rationalized, she'd done something wrong.

It was hard to believe that the Brad who played Early was the same one who'd so recently been Paul Maclean. There was nothing golden about this character. He shambled, he looked small and quite ordinary. But, as events unfolded, so did Early. His command and control of the situation grew. He was uneducated, a slob, but he knew things; he understood them. He was cunning. And Brad was able to put that across. He had charisma. Underneath the beard and the leering grin was a very powerful magnet.

There was a touch of Charles Manson in Brad's portrayal—in the slightly off-center stare, the manic edge his monologues could take.

But even when he was looking quite deliberately ugly and a bit overweight, Brad could still make hearts beat faster among the women on the set, as director Dominic Sena amazedly told *People* magazine: "This guy just gets through to women, no matter what."

Perhaps it was unfortunate that his sexiness didn't make it on to the screen; the movie might have fared better at the box office. The *New York Times* wasn't impressed or convinced, saying that "*Kalifornia* . . . lets its stars overact to the rafters as it vacillates between wild pretentiousness and occasional high style" and judged that it was "badly lacking a moral compass." *Variety* had some of the same reservations ("somewhat overplayed and coy about its destination") but was able to see the film's merits: "The film . . . packs a wallop and should do solid business on the specialized circuit."

However, both critics were able to agree that director Sena had made it look very good. *Variety* noted that it was "an extremely handsome production imbued with a chilling surrealistic sensibility," while the *New York Times* conceded that "*Kalifornia* is indeed good-looking, with its striking desert landscapes."

The reviewers were also ready to agree that Brad had put on a bravura performance. "Mr. Pitt lends nasty credence to Early's viciousness," the *New York Times* enthused, continuing, "*Kalifornia* confirms that Mr. Pitt is an interesting, persuasive actor." In *Variety*, Leonard Klady wrote that "the charismatic Pitt explores his character with quiet resolve, venting both horror and darkly comic implications."

For Klady, though, "Lewis steals the show with an affectless performance that registers pity, pathos and pluck."

The reality was that for both Brad and Juliette, *Kalifornia* was the best work they'd both done to date. It was not the most attractive, but that was where the skill came in, to make it all seem real.

To justify stepping back from certain super stardom, at least for a little while, Brad had to offer something special. *Kalifornia* was it. Early was pure menace, thinly overlayed with a rough, down-home charm. From time to time, often without provocation, the violence would shoot through. He was a volcano, constantly on the edge of blowing. The intensity involved in maintaining Early's edge was a physical and mental drain on Brad.

Very few actors, particularly those rising as fast as Brad, would have been willing to consider the part. Playing someone as unrepentantly awful as Early was hardly a career move guaranteed to win more fans.

But that had been part of Brad's attraction to the role. Brad hadn't courted publicity or fame. Quite the opposite; he kept trying to keep them at bay by taking "unsuitable" roles like Early or Johnny Suede, projects that would let him develop outside the spotlight. What remained first and foremost in his mind was that he was an *actor*, not a screen personality. So, he took the best, the most challenging work that was offered to him, whether it was big-budget Hollywood or a shoestring independent production.

"Could I have played the good guy in *Kalifornia*?" he mused some time later. "Sure. But

I needed the balance. I don't believe in the 'all-your-eggs-in-one-bucket' kind of theory. You get pushed in this business, you just gotta push back harder. Because it comes down to you. I mean, people got different takes on things, people got good takes. But only you know about your own deal—your own creation, right?"

That idea made him very much an anomaly in a business where the emphasis had always been on career and money. But it fit in perfectly with the way Brad was developing—if it felt right, then it was the right choice. The artistic decisions were the important ones; the rest would take care of itself.

To be fair, Brad was in the position to be able to take that attitude. Work was coming to him; he had few financial worries. But it was remarkably refreshing for him to want to make the most of his ability, rather than just bolster his ego.

Of course, no sooner had he wrapped up work on *Kalifornia* than scripts about serial killers began piling up in his mailbox.

"You take a movie because there's something it brings to you that you want to investigate," Brad explained in *Vanity Fair*. "I felt like I'd done the serial killer guy, and everything was kind of going in that direction. And I wanted to go to a place where somebody cared about something, you know? Gave a shit about something."

He'd picked the toughest roles he could find. Not that he would have had it any other way, really. There was an excitement, a rush that Brad felt when he took on a character and began to live him. Not that that didn't create some problems.

"Somewhere in the third or fourth week [of shooting], you respond to things a little differently, like your character would respond," he said. "I don't like it. I can't wait to get my own clothes back on, listen to some good music, eat what I want to eat," he said.

It might have made life difficult, but the fact that Brad could submerge himself so deeply in his characters meant that he gave the best performances. Early Grayce had been a complete tour de force, quite unforgettable. Brad's need to continually prove himself, and be taken as much more than a gorgeous face, surely had been satisfied with this.

In many ways the role marked the end of an era for Brad. He'd been able to start work on *Kalifornia* before *A River Runs Through It* appeared. Once that was out, there was no real chance to turn back, or to take the small films that satisfied his artistic impulses. With that film he had become a full-fledged star, wined, dined, and given the royal treatment by producers and studios. He was the leading man to watch now.

Success came to him at the right time. He'd had a chance to work his way up the ladder, to hone his craft and become mature enough to take the sudden, effusive praise with a large pinch of salt.

But Brad wasn't quite ready to abandon his film freedom for the restrictions and rewards of stardom. There was one thing he wanted to do yet. . . .

Quentin Tarantino was the new toast of Hollywood, both as a director and a writer. After his "discovery" and the making of his first feature, the violent *Reservoir Dogs*, there was a huge rush for his old scripts. One had turned into gold; who knew what the rest might contain?

The first to see the light of day was *True Romance*. Again, it was extremely violent, but it had a goofy, almost cartoonish undercurrent that paid homage to any number of classic thrillers. Tony Scott (brother of Ridley, who'd done *Thelma & Louise*) was picked to direct, with Christian Slater and Patricia Arquette set to star.

Such was Tarantino-mania in the industry, though, that anyone who was anyone wanted a part, large, small, or cameo. Dennis Hopper, Christopher Walken, Gary Oldman, Samuel L. Jackson, Val Kilmer—the list went on and on. Brad, too, wanted in on it.

It was pleasure, nothing more, that led him to take the role of Floyd, the stoned slacker roommate of Slater's best friend.

"That was fun," he recalled later. "But I was only there for a couple of days."

The fun certainly came across. He only had a few lines, hidden behind the long hair of a wig (although very soon his own hair would be that long), but he put across those lines perfectly. The quizzical look, the slurred speech, the effusive hippie friendliness—all were exact and real. But that was to be expected, really. Brad might have been playing the role for his own enjoyment, but he was enough of a perfectionist to want his portrayal to be absolutely right. It didn't matter whether Floyd was dealing with friends, hit men, or Mafia bigwigs, he was pleasant and polite, offering them a hit off the bong and a place to watch television (seemingly his two major pastimes).

It was easy and an ideal, upbeat way to emerge from the deep, exhausting shoot of *Kalifornia*. Floyd was the perfect antidote to the warped mind of Early Grayce. As *Variety* wrote, "there's dopey fun in Brad Pitt's space cadet."

But for him it wasn't about the reviews. Brad would almost as soon have had his appearance anonymous and uncredited, to let everyone wonder if that was really him. Of course, the studio wasn't about to let that happen. Every big name on the poster was a few more tickets sold.

No, it was about a few laughs, some light relief after three years of very intense work that had been draining, both physically and emotionally. Now it was time for Brad to take a break, regain a sense of who *he* was, and look at his options for the future. There were massive changes happening, and decisions to be made. One of them promised to be very difficult indeed.

Brad and Juliette had been an established

couple for three years, almost a lifetime by Hollywood standards. They'd seen their lives altered far beyond their wildest expectations, from faint recognition to budding superstardom. But they'd established a bond that seemed solid enough to last a long, long time. They were too busy for the wild life, and neither seemed too inclined to it, anyway. For them the chance to stay at home, catch up, maybe entertain some friends and play some music, was more than enough. The house on Beechwood Canyon was small and unpretentious by the standards of their new fame, but it was ample for their needs. Brad's antiques were carefully displayed; Juliette's vintage clothing filled the closets.

They were opposites who meshed together well. Brad was completely laid-back and tidy while Juliette remained driven and intense, leaving a clutter of clothes and books and everything in her wake. They loved each other. But, as a source told the *National Enquirer*, "she became very intense about their relationship and Brad became scared when she started to tell friends that they would soon marry."

That was a step he wasn't quite ready to

take yet. It was *too* serious, too much of a commitment to make. He wanted to marry someday, just not now. But it was, supposedly, what she wanted, and he just couldn't give it. So, after completing his few days' filming on *True Romance* in February 1993, he told Juliette that he wanted to end things.

"To say Juliette's heart was broken is to make the understatement of the year," an insider said.

"I still love the woman," Brad said, long after it was over, explaining his actions. "There's some real genius there. I had a great time with her.... She has her own views, and I respected those views. She does know people. It was one of the greatest relationships I've ever been in. The problem is, we grow up with this vision that love conquers all, and that's just not so, is it?"

Part of the problem was the difference in ages. Brad was almost thirty, while Juliette was still only nineteen. She understood a lot about people, but was still looking at the world through the rose-colored glasses of youth. Brad, older, somewhat wiser, believed things were just fine as they stood; they were happy, and so why change things? But once

Juliette started pressing for marriage, and he said no, there's no need, a turning point had been reached. He knew she'd always have that small edge of resentment, and possibly distrust, that would color and eventually wreck the relationship. On top of that, if he wasn't willing to give her what she wanted, wasn't it fairer to leave her free to find it? It was honest, and, as Brad put it "I'd say I try to guide my life by honesty. And that's a hard thing."

They talked for a long time, going back and forth. It was sad and terrible for both of them to see three years vanish so quickly. It was the only way, though; they'd gone too far to kiss and make up. There were tears from both of them.

Brad said he'd move out. It was the good thing, the right thing. He was ending it, putting her through all the heartbreak. She liked the house. He'd find somewhere else.

Although he could afford it, he didn't immediately look for a place to buy. Things were too up in the air to consider any type of permanence yet. It was better to rent a house.

He moved his possessions, the furniture, the espresso machine, the CDs, and guitars into the new place. But it didn't feel right. Brad couldn't seem to relax there the way he needed; it just wasn't home. So at night he found himself going out, driving down the hills, along the inner city streets where there were people and life. Often he'd go on to a club, and sit at the bar drinking beers and smoking Camels, listening to a band. And meeting women.

"The main reason I used to go to bars was to pick up girls," he confessed later. Not that he really had much work to do; they flocked to him. He had his choice.

Brad should have felt better. He was young, handsome to the point of being beautiful, and a star. But in reality it was an empty time. He and Juliette had been together so long, and the pain of parting was still very raw.

So the nights were long, a mixture of music, a few beers, driving around until the sky began to lighten. Or, if he didn't go out, hour upon hour of very bad movies on cable. It was his way of coping with his pain.

It didn't help that he wasn't working. Brad had always defined himself as an actor, so to be sitting around day after day left him curiously incomplete. He needed the rest, there was no doubt about that, but inactivity didn't come easy to him. He'd grown so used to being busy that the time weighed very heavily on his hands.

Projects were being considered. Now that Brad was a star, he needed something suitable, a *big* movie that would bring him even further into the public eye. There were offers, but they were never quite the right thing. So Brad continued to fret.

At a party he met an actress, Jitka Pohlodek, who was supposedly from Czechoslovakia "by way of Arkansas," and whom he affectionately nicknamed Yit. There was enough of the southerner in her to make him laugh, yet she seemed exotic enough to be intriguing; after all, she kept two bobcats as pets. And she was pretty. The two began seeing each other regularly. Life grew a little better.

Then, finally, the call came from his agent. They'd found not one, but two great movies. Was Brad interested in reading the scripts?

He couldn't wait.

Eight

The first script he unwrapped was for *Legends of the Fall*. The movie was being put together by Edward Zwick and Marshall Herskovitz, who'd been the team behind the television show *thirtysomething*. They knew Brad would be a big draw, not so much from *A River Runs Through It*, but from the stir he'd created on the TV show.

As soon as Brad read the script, it struck a deep chord with him. This was something he really wanted to be a part of.

"This story was one of the only ones where I've ever said, 'I'm the guy for this one,' " he told *Premiere*. "This story I felt like I knew from the beginning to the end. I knew the stops and I knew the turns. This one meant more."

He was so convinced that the film should be made—with him in it—that he was even willing to defer part of his reported $3 million salary, becoming Zwick's partner in the production company.

With that interest, TriStar was willing to look very seriously at backing the film. Then, when Sir Anthony Hopkins agreed to join the cast, that clinched the deal. TriStar was definitely in, committed to a $30 million budget.

But, although *Legends of the Fall* was filmed before *Interview with the Vampire,* it was *Interview* that reached theaters first and made Brad into a full-fledged celebrity.

Brad was the first choice for Louis, according to director Neil Jordan, who said, "I saw everything he's done and he is just absolutely captivating."

Casting Lestat proved a little more difficult. Names were bandied around, including Mel Gibson, Ralph Fiennes, and Billy Baldwin. The part was even offered to Daniel Day-Lewis, who turned it down, feeling that he didn't like what it would do to him. At the time Brad thought that was "more actor bullshit," but by the time the filming was over, he was willing to concede that he had an idea what Day-Lewis had been talking about. The book had impressed him, he thought the movie was excellent, and he was proud of his work in it, but, he said, "It's just that for me, making the movie wasn't so great."

That was perfectly understandable. Without any kind of break, he moved from the long, draining, very physical shoot of *Legends* to *Interview,* walking into a production that had been mired in problems from the word go.

Anne Rice's novel, *Interview with the Vampire,* had long been a best-selling favorite, but every attempt to bring it to the screen had failed. Rice herself had written a script, but whatever strategy was tried (one of which had been a musical by Elton John, another a drama with John Travolta as Lestat), things never managed to fall into place until 1989, when David Geffen took over the project. Then more time passed—three years, to be exact.

Neil Jordan, fresh from his success with *The Crying Game,* was brought in as director. The casting began. As soon as Tom Cruise signed for the movie, Rice was in a fury, declaring publicly that she couldn't imagine anyone making a worse portrayal of her cherished vampire Lestat than Cruise.

"He's a cute kid," she announced, "on top of the world and on his way to becoming a great actor, but I'm not sure he knows what he's getting into. . . . [He] should do himself a favor and withdraw."

But he didn't. Jordan and Cruise stuck to their guns. Then, just before filming was about to begin, River Phoenix, who was to play the interviewer, died in Los Angeles of a drug overdose. It seemed, quite menacingly, as if the movie was cursed.

Rice's script was taken apart, and, reportedly, much of it rewritten by Jordan, which caused more acrimony between writer and filmmakers.

This was the situation Brad walked into. He was tired, completely exhausted really, after his strenuous work on *Legends of the Fall,* and needed a rest, a break of some kind, but the schedules just couldn't be juggled to allow it.

It was a huge change, to go from a production which was largely filmed in the open, among the wide skies of the Canadian Rockies, to the claustrophobia of sets and soundstages, no matter how elaborate, and a series of nighttime exteriors in New Orleans, Paris, and San Francisco.

Brad had known Tristan, understood him in his bones. Louis was a completely different matter. Living forever with guilt, wanting to die but not able to, conjuring those up every day was a constant struggle, not just as an actor, but as a human being. The emotions invaded his system, and left him depressed and confused. This supposedly caused some conflict between Brad and his co-star, Tom Cruise, although that always has been widely denied.

"I didn't realize there were any rumors about Brad and Tom not getting along," Neil Jordan said later.

Brad would add, "I tell you, the machine Tom runs is quite impressive. . . . I like the guy . . . but at a point I started really resenting him. In retrospect I realize that it was completely because of who our characters were. I realize that it was my problem."

It also arose from a difference in attitude. Brad, of course, was laid-back and relaxed, while, by all accounts, Cruise was wanting a lot of control, demanding a closed set, and reputedly asking for platform shoes so he would be as tall as Brad.

But the film was made, slowly and excruciatingly. For Brad it was a grind.

"I hated doing this movie. Hated it. My character is depressed from the beginning to the end. Five and a half months of that is too much." As he added later, "I don't like when a movie messes with your day."

Interview with the Vampire messed with many of his days. Not needed for a few days during filming in Paris, he slipped across the Channel for a few days, a short roadtrip to Scotland to restore his equanimity.

Although Cruise was the nominal star, *Interview with the Vampire* was just as much Brad's film. Cruise played Lestat, the French vampire who traveled to America literally in search of fresh blood, a companion for his endless nights. In 1791 New Orleans he found him in Louis (Brad), a young plantation owner with no will to live after the death of his wife.

Once he was initiated, Louis began to regret his decision; it was death, not eternal life as a beautiful young man, that he wanted. But death was impossible. Nor could he bring himself to kill other humans for their blood—he tried to subsist only on rats.

Under Lestat's constant goading, he finally gave way, but always in anguish. Lestat relished the sport of it, but Louis remained reluctant and full of pain. He tried to kill a young girl whose mother had died, but bungled the attempt. Lestat brought her to their apartment, where she, too, became a vampire.

For a while Louis was happy. With the girl to pamper, someone who was almost a daughter, life began to seem worthwhile again. But Claudia proved to have a far more voracious appetite than either of her adult companions.

For many years the three lived together, an often uneasy triangle. Claudia's mind and emotions grew, but her body could never be more than that of a ten-year-old child. However she might try, she couldn't change her appearance.

Still Lestat wanted them around for their companionship.

Finally they killed him—or so they thought—and embarked on a journey to Paris. It had been Lestat's home; surely there would be other vampires there, people who might be able to answer all the questions Louis and

Claudia had about their kind.

There *were* others there, although it took the pair a long time to find them. Finally there came an invitation to the "vampire theatre," a performance in an old church. The vampires proved to be real, an aristocratic band under the leadership of Armand (Antonio Banderas). The group destroyed Claudia by exposing her to sunlight, and tried to wall up Louis before Armand freed him.

Louis's revenge was terrible. He set fire to the crypt where they lived, hacking their bodies as they flew out of the coffins where they were sleeping.

Armand tried to console him, to inject some joy and purpose into him, but for Louis there could be no consolation. Louis wandered. Time passed into the twentieth century and the modern age. He returned to New Orleans, yearning for home. There he encountered, once again, Lestat.

Lestat was older, more philosophical, weaker, living in an age he couldn't adapt to or understand. Lestat asked Louis to rejoin him, although he obviously knew what the answer would be. Louis was still heartsick, still conscience-stricken, but the world had opened up for him.

Louis moved on to San Francisco, where he made contact with a journalist, Malloy (Christian Slater), and offered him the story of his life. Not surprisingly, the interviewer was skeptical of his claims until Louis offered him proof. That was how the story was told, in flashbacks that took up from Louis's narration.

The writer was young and didn't understand the burden and sadness of a life that could never end. Instead, to him, it was exciting, a thrilling prospect. Louis, who knew the life's harsh reality all too well, told him to leave.

In his car, crossing the Golden Gate Bridge, the journalist began to play the tapes he'd made. What he didn't know was that Lestat was waiting in the back, having followed Louis from New Orleans. He pounced, biting, and offering the same choice he'd given Louis two hundred years earlier—death or eternal life.

Once Anne Rice saw Cruise as Lestat, she was quick to apologize, even taking out a two-page print ad to say how wonderful she thought he was in the role. This turnabout was intriguing to many people, and dragged them off their couches to the theaters just to see what all of it was about. Further controversy fuelled the flames when Oprah Winfrey walked out of a special screening, saying the film was too violent. It just increased the audiences. They added themselves to the Rice fans, the Cruise fans, and the rapidly growing number of Brad Pitt devotees who packed the cinemas to see *Interview with the Vampire.* On its first weekend alone, the movie grossed $38.7 million, the fourth largest debut in history.

It was a beautiful, expensive production, lovingly filmed in nocturnal blues and blacks and greens. All the reviews were quick to mention that. But almost all the critics disliked the movie. For *New York*'s David Denby it was "exceptionally boring, parochial, and remote." Julie Salamon, writing in the *Wall Street Journal,* commented, "I don't get it. . . . I was unmoved by the story." *Rolling Stone* was "dazzled but unmoved." The *New Yorker* felt that director Jordan's "virtuosity can't disguise the movie's emptiness."

Nor were they any kinder to the actors. The

writers were generally willing to say that Tom Cruise was better than they'd expected, after which they criticized him for not being good enough. There seemed to be the beginnings of a Brad Pitt backlash in the words written about him. Again, David Denby seemed to lead the pack: "As for Brad Pitt, different vampires may tell him he's beautiful, but actually he looks awkward in period costume—an unsmiling, inhibited actor with puffy lips and a dead voice." In *Commonweal*, Richard Alleva wrote that "Brad Pitt . . . comes closer to success as Louis, a role that doesn't encompass the flamboyant extremes of Lestat's behavior. But Pitt, too, is betrayed by his voice. . . . He sounds like a little boy trying to imitate some childish idea of how a great actor declaims."

America called Brad's screen presence "wooden," continuing that it was "all the more stupefying because Neil Jordan attempts to portray him as the objective, dispassionate narrator of the horrors that he witnesses and precipitates." At least *Newsweek* was willing to concede that Brad had "the hardest role and the hardest time" before adding that "his sullen, inarticulate style can be distractingly contemporary."

Time, however, saw beyond that.

"The movie really belongs to Brad Pitt," Brian D. Johnson wrote, "who turns in a beautifully measured yet passionate performance in the central role of Louis, the reluctant vampire."

Unfortunately, his was almost the only voice raised in Brad's defense by the press. But David Geffen, the film's producer, was quick to agree. "Brad's character [in the movie] is very passive. You need an awful lot of charisma to be in a movie where someone else does all the action. And Brad has it."

Indeed he did. If *A River Runs Through It* had left him looking like a star, with plenty of people wanting to see more of him, *Interview with the Vampire* truly consolidated his celebrity status.

In all fairness, the character he played helped the image. Louis might have been a vampire, but he was a romantic through and through, yearning for death after the loss of his wife. He felt guilt about having to take life. It was a role full of sadness and yearning. Above all, the long hair falling to his shoulders and framing his face honestly suited Brad. If it was possible, the style made him even better looking. Certainly legions of new fans thought so. To them he was an ideal—gorgeous, reserved, with aristocratic manners and an air of mystery and sorrow. Many of those who paid again and again to see the film weren't there to see the Gothic trappings of vampirism or Tom Cruise murdering everything in his path—they went to swoon over Brad's performance.

He really did bring something perfect to the role. Talking with Malloy, the interviewer, his empty tone was exactly right. He'd lived for so long and lost everything he loved, with no end in sight, that he'd naturally come to take a detached view of the world. That was what Brad captured. In the flashbacks his anguish was real.

"His emotions are all right there on the surface," was how Tom Cruise summarized Brad's portrayal. Which was how it should have been. Louis wasn't an intellectual or a man of artificial passions. He wasn't tremendously articulate. Once Lestat had given him the dubious gift of eternal life, he found himself torn in two.

That put Brad into his element of being able to convey emotions with very few words.

They played across his face constantly—doubt, anger, longing, and, once they'd been joined by the child, Claudia, there was even joy for a while—leaving him more transparent than his skin would eventually become.

The reality was that Brad had given a remarkable performance, as Anne Rice herself commented in a newsletter circulated to "Vampire Chronicle" fans: "The Barbie Doll from Hell (her nickname for Brad) was a hell of a Louis in *Interview*, upturned nose and all ... he was beautiful as Louis, how fortunate we were."

That lost, romantic beauty that Brad gave Louis formed a strong part of the film's success. It would have done well at the box office anyway, there was never much doubt about that, but Brad's appearance truly sent it over the top. Ironically, though, *People* magazine, which would soon be crowning him "The Sexiest Man Alive," barely gave him a mention in its review of the movie. Not that his presence was missed. The crowds were already out, the lines at the theaters. As before, the raves about Brad spread by word of mouth. He was becoming a superstar in spite of the critics.

What the writers didn't understand, women

did. Brad simply exuded charisma, a magnetism that was just irresistible. Even exhausted, in a role that gave him constant trouble, it was there. It leapt through the screen and enveloped you. You simply couldn't take your eyes off of him.

It was what he'd already done in *Thelma & Louise, A River Runs Through It,* and, to a greater or lesser extent, all the movies he'd been in. He had the power to enthrall. The camera loved him, and so did audiences.

If it was obvious to people willing to pay money, then why not the critics? It was hard to believe they were so jaded that they were immune to his charm. Perhaps they were jealous of his popularity, and saw in him—quite wrongly—another phenomenon of The Face and The Body.

Which may have been why most people wanted him, but it was hardly what *he* was about. A beautiful face could only take him so far. Beyond that—and Brad had definitely moved well beyond that—it depended on his ability as an actor. No director would be so foolish as to hire someone who looked good but couldn't act for such a complex picture as *Interview with the Vampire.* At least, not if he was interested in working in Hollywood again.

The Face and The Body were the initial attractions about Brad, but they were hardly the only ones. Anyone who really looked at him saw beyond those. Still, it made it much easier to quickly write him off for the critics, who didn't want to recognize the phenomenon that was going on right before their eyes.

Brad wasn't just a movie star. What he'd become, without any of the usual hype of a publicity machine, was the man of the age. It had happened before, with Clark Gable, James Dean, and Robert Redford. He had the qualities that summed up the time. Beyond looks, that was what people saw in him.

He was vulnerable, somewhat tongue-tied, masculine without ever being macho or threatening. He could be a friend as well as a lover. He might not say much, but he still showed his emotions. Those qualities were sexy, and they were him, and they shone through in the roles that he played. That had as much, if not more, to do with why people loved him. People came away from the theater with a feeling that they knew him and understood him.

Of course, that wasn't quite the case. It wasn't as simple as that. There were elements of himself in Brad's performances, which was only natural, since he drew what he could from within himself. But those elements hardly made up the whole picture.

It was like an iceberg. The on-screen Brad was only one tiny part of the whole, and the rest remained largely hidden in his private life. But now, more than ever before, there was a huge groundswell of people wanting to know about that, to get a glimpse inside. They loved him and they wanted to know more.

That was difficult for him. His private life had always been exactly that. There'd been press interest after *A River Runs Through It* when he suddenly became hot, but that was a trickle compared to the deluge of requests that were coming in to his publicist now. It seemed like half the journalists in America wanted their slice of Brad.

The problem was that Brad didn't really want to reveal all. Talking about himself just wasn't his way. Nor was badmouthing other people, or dishing the dirt. Off-screen he wanted to be as anonymous as he could, which was rapidly becoming impossible. He didn't want to become another personality to be collected.

It wasn't a case of being contrary or aloof. He genuinely saw himself as an actor and nothing more. The more people knew about *him,* the harder it would become for people to watch him in a film and see who he was portraying. He could make it look easy and totally natural, but it was difficult work, and when he was away from it he needed to be able to disappear, to be himself. To be able to do that, he had to keep that separate, out of the public eye.

But the requests kept coming, and he couldn't keep turning them all down. So he met with reporters, people from *Rolling Stone, Vanity Fair,* and *Premiere.* But he talked about his films, and when he discussed himself, he did it obliquely, never really opening up and letting everything out. He was polite, but guarded.

It wasn't any kind of calculated technique meant to intensify the mystery about Brad Pitt. Really, it was just another part of his upbringing coming out: You didn't talk about yourself to strangers. It was presumptuous. Never mind if that was why they'd come—it was rude.

In a way it was funny. He'd become America's new symbol of sex and romance, an actor whose asking price for a movie seemed to be rising every day. His life had changed beyond recognition. He could have had any woman he chose, gone wherever he wanted, done almost anything. Underneath it all, the exterior that seemed a little strange, a little disconnected, he was still the good southern boy Bill and Jane Pitt had raised him to be.

It was certainly refreshing, even if the journalists found it frustrating. In a tabloid age where the national impulse seemed to be to reveal all, here was someone who was keeping his dignity. Where he had nothing nice to say, he kept his mouth shut. More than that, unlike most celebrities, fame hadn't gone to his head. There was no history of temper tantrums, substance abuse, or scandal. Brad lived his life on his own terms, within a certain set of rules, beholden to no one.

Of course, not really talking about himself made him all the more intriguing. Everyone wanted to know who he really was. But there wasn't any deep secret; he was who he was. Like everyone, he had his problems, but he coped with them.

The truth was that Brad saw things as essentially quite simple, as he explained to one interviewer. "When things get out of hand, there's a simple answer. Some people are good at finding it quickly, some never find it."

Brad, it seemed, was one of those who was good at finding the answer quickly.

He knew he was popular, and he knew why. It had all spiraled out of any sort of control. Even if he'd tried, Brad couldn't have controlled it.

Frankly, with *Interview with the Vampire* out of the way, it didn't matter any more. Whatever happened would happen. He was exhausted. Filming two movies back-to-back, particularly two long, punishing shoots like these had been, had just drained him. He needed some time at home to shake off the roles and rediscover himself. Playing Louis had been uncomfortable, sometimes even disturbing.

Jitka and her bobcats were waiting for him, but coming home and looking at her, he realized it just wasn't working. He wasn't ready for it yet. He needed to make more changes in his life, and she was one of the things he'd have to leave behind.

"I love you a lot," he reportedly told her, "but I hate to feel crowded."

It was time for Brad to move on again, and this time to somewhere with more permanence, a place he could really call home. Now that he was fully established in Hollywood, he felt the need for some roots there, a house.

It didn't take long to find the ideal one. It was small, a 1910 Crafstman once owned by horror-show hostess Elvira, a place with beautiful details, like built-in glass cabinets and plenty of exposed wood. It felt comfortable. And the antiques he'd collected—the Tiffany lamps, the tables and chairs—could have been made for the place.

Even better, it was set in several acres, hidden away in its own little world of terraces and surprises. There was a pool, of course, but turn another corner, and suddenly there was a pond. Move away and there was a cave that someone had carefully constructed.

It was ideal, a sort of wonderland where he could explore and feel like a kid again or just relax and hide from the world. Palm trees and bougainvillea covered the hillside, shielding the place from prying eyes. Then, when he discovered the property had a music connection, that it had once been owned by Chas Chandler, Jimi Hendrix's manager, he knew it was perfect, even meant to be. He bought it immediately.

"It's kind of special to me, really sacred," he affirmed after moving in. All his possessions might still be in boxes and the house needed plenty of work, but he felt a sense of peace creeping through him.

The house wasn't his only purchase. There were the six hundred acres in the Ozarks back home, where he could get away from the world and refresh himself in the good air he'd grown up with. It was close enough to where the rest of his family still lived that they could use it too. Property is wealth, an old saying goes, and Brad was starting to listen to the old sayings.

For now, though, Brad contented himself with unpacking, setting up a home in the midst of a constant stream of workmen. He moved in the forty chameleons he and Yit had bought, their cages looking like odd Chinese lanterns in the yard. Then, as the finishing touch, to really make the place his, he acquired three dogs, Purty, Todd Potter, and Saudi. He'd always wanted them, big dogs, active and playful, but he'd never lived anywhere with enough room enough before. Here they could roam and run as much as they pleased, and so could Brad.

He felt content.

Nine

If *Interview with the Vampire* brought Brad into the front rank of movie idols and hunks, *Legends of the Fall* sent the world crazy for him.

It was only to be expected. Tristan was an incredibly romantic, tragic figure, the center of a story full of love, heartbreak, joy, and sadness—all the extremes of emotion. As Brad explained it, Tristan was about "sinking below, rising above, going off, giving up, taking charge, taking control. This man's journey seemed very accurate to me and very true."

The part could have been written for him. Even Jim Harrison, who wrote the novella on which the film was based, was impressed. "He never gives the appearance of trying to think of what to say next. So your attention is focused completely on him."

It was also the first movie Brad had been involved with in any capacity beyond acting, which gave him a greater impetus to make it the very best it could be. Much of that would come from the casting. He and Anthony Hopkins were already set, but what about the other brothers and Susannah?

Brad had one suggestion—Aidan Quinn as Alfred, the oldest brother. The two had never met, but Brad was familiar with his work and realized he would bring a real nobility to the role.

"It could easily have gone wimpy," Brad said, "and we needed someone who'd be equal to Tristan . . . and that's Aidan."

Producer Ed Zwick agreed.

"As good as everyone is in the movie, Aidan's part is the hardest. And consequently, it's the part that holds the movie together. He is *us*."

Then Henry Thomas, now all grown up from his part as the boy in *E.T.* was hired to play youngest brother Samuel Ludlow, and, following a rushed screen test, English actress

Julia Ormond, who'd impressed Zwick with her acting in the HBO television movie *Stalin,* signed as Susannah. Everything was rolling.

Although, like *A River Runs Through It,* the film was set in Montana in the wild country beyond Helena, the shooting was done in the even wilder landscape of the Canadian Rockies outside Calgary.

There was one great problem built into the production from the beginning. with Brad already committed to *Interview with the Vampire,* his time on the set was limited. He had to be finished by a certain date, which meant that his scenes had to be shot first. And they had to be right. There could be no going back and reshooting. It created pressure.

Sometimes the lid blew off. There were reports of conflicts between Brad and director Zwick.

"Sure, we went at it," Zwick admitted, "and that is part of the process." Brad, on the other hand, was glad it happened.

"It's good if two people care," he said. "Have at it, 'cause at the end you're going to come up with something good."

In spite of those occasional problems, it was a relaxed, friendly shoot. As always, Brad was his polite self, always going out of his way to thank the crew for their work, never acting like a star but just a regular guy. His only concession to his status was to rent a house, which he shared—quite platonically—with Julia Ormond. Often, when the week's work was complete, a number of people involved with the film would go up there with their instruments to relax, drink a few beers, have a jam session, and laugh. Brad invited his brother Doug up to visit for a couple of weeks, and so a member of the family was able to see first-hand that the stardom hadn't gone to Brad's head.

Of course the papers made the most of Brad's living arrangement, milking it for all its possibilities, but neither Brad nor Julia really cared.

"We knew that was coming," he said afterwards. "Sooner or later. It was completely about convenience. It's been nice."

Of course, the two had their opportunity to be close enough on-screen as their characters finally gave in to each other one night. The scene was filmed on a freezing ice curling rink just outside Calgary, the bed set up on a plywood set.

"It's not the most romantic setting, you

know?" Brad laughed later. "Very anti-erection, if I can say that."

But he did what he could to add some romance to the moment, bringing in a boom box and playing Toad the Wet Sprocket's album *Fear* as background music—a trick he'd learned from Ridley Scott during his scene with Geena Davis in *Thelma & Louise*. But even now, his main concern was exactly the same as it had been then—"my poor mom!" Some things seemed unlikely ever to change.

The story followed the Ludlow family through almost three quarters of a century. The Colonel (Hopkins), disgusted by the way the government was treating Indians, resigned his commission, and set about building a ranch in the Montana wilderness. His wife, unable to stand the place, returned to Boston after delivering three sons, who stayed with their father and his Indian companion and friend, One Stab.

The boys all learned Indian ways, but it was Tristan, the middle brother, who took them to heart, fighting and wounding (and being wounded by) a bear when still young.

The youngest son, Samuel Thomas, went away to Harvard and returned with a fianceé,

Susannah (Ormond), with whom the other brothers immediately fell in love. But any chance of lasting happiness was shattered by the declaration of World War I. Samuel decided to go to Canada and enlist, and the other two went along to protect him.

They would have succeeded, but Samuel volunteered for a mission while Alfred was in the hospital and Tristan wasn't around. Samuel died, and Tristan promised a nightmarish vengeance on his killers, before cutting out his brother's heart in the Indian manner, so his spirit could go free.

Alfred, wounded, returned to America where he proposed to Susannah. She turned him down. But when Tristan eventually arrived, the attraction between the two of them became too powerful to deny. It was a time of joy for them both, but it couldn't last; Susannah was never really his. He had to go. She promised she would wait, forever if necessary.

But forever proved too long. While Tristan traveled the wild parts of the globe, Susannah gave in and married Alfred, who, thanks to the corrupt O'Bannion forces in the town of Helena, had become a congressman.

Meanwhile, the ranch was falling to pieces.

The Colonel had had a stroke, there was no money coming in. When Tristan finally reappeared, expecting to find everything the same, he received a sobering shock. Now he was ready to settle down, but he was going to be denied the chance.

With his father's blessing, he took to bootlegging, defying the people who controlled Alfred's career. He also married Isabel Two, the half-Indian girl who'd always loved him, and who'd grown into a beautiful young woman. They had two sons; he grew to love her. But peace wouldn't come so readily for Tristan. Ambushed by Alfred's political puppeteers, a stray bullet killed Isabel. Tristan beat the shooter until he was close to death, but that was hardly satisfying. Susannah, realizing that her love for Tristan—and the fact she was living a lie—was responsible for so much of the violence, committed suicide.

Revenge, when it came, was brutal. The people responsible for Isabel Two's murder were killed. Though there was no evidence against the Ludlow family, that didn't stop the O'Bannions, with their pet sheriff, from coming to the ranch. There would be no trial, no exposing the truth. They just wanted Tristan dead.

It almost happened. But the family, for the first time in years, pulled together. The Colonel took the first shot, and Alfred, in a final rebellion against his masters, took the last.

But Tristan still wasn't completely free. Others would come looking for him with their guns. He left for the north woods, and lived there until he was in his sixties. He had another encounter with the bear, this time a fatal one. By then it was time. He was ready to make a good death.

Again, the critics weren't enthusiastic about the film. The *Christian Science Monitor* felt there wasn't "a speck of genuine feeling in its glossy images," and *People* said "it either sweeps you up in its rapturous emotional wake or . . . you just sit there and snicker." *Rolling Stone* wrote that it was aimed at mall audiences, who "take their movies like their buttered popcorn—in sweet, nutrient-free puffs that go down easy," and the *Wall Street Journal* called it an "overblown oater. . . . I felt as if I were trapped in a Ralph Lauren infomercial."

Only the *New Republic* took it seriously, and even then decided that "besides the structural jig-sawing, the dialogue is inadequate—

windy in the 'epic' moments, trite in the intimate ones; so the theme isn't realized nearly as well as is needed."

To a point, Brad agreed with them. What was released had changed somewhat from the movie he agreed to make.

"By taking out as much as they did, the movie becomes too mushy," he said after the movie had been edited. "If I'd known where it was going to end up, I'd have fought against the cheese. . . . This is a good movie. There are just moments where, if it was reduced to that, if that's all we were going to see of him, I would have whittled it down. I wouldn't have shown so much."

Not that it mattered to the audiences. As soon as it opened, rushed out at Christmas 1994 to be eligible for Oscar nominations (although, in the end, it didn't receive any), it immediately became one of the top box office hits. People were eager to see Brad, and there he was, larger than life and twice as gorgeous. His long hair flowed, his smile, shy and seductive at the same time, made the movie completely irresistible. The fact that it was an incredibly romantic tearjerker only helped matters; as a beautiful tragic hero, there couldn't have been a better role for Brad to cement his stardom.

"You know, *Legends of the Fall* was great," he said. "It's been the hardest thing I tried to tackle, and as I look back . . . it's been good."

But the critics were generally as unkind to him as they were to the movie. *People* found that "sometimes his portrayal of a man at war with himself is moving; at other times, he seems to be all attitude" while the *Dallas Observer* decided that "Pitt doesn't emote nearly as well as he pouts—even though the two are, for him, often inseparable."

But *Rolling Stone* was willing to admit that "Pitt carries the picture. The blue-eyed boy who seemed a bit lost in *Interview with the Vampire* proves himself a bona fide movie star, stealing every scene he's in." Siskel and Ebert said his performance was "star-making," which seemed a little odd, since he was already a major star. And on *Good Morning America,* Joel Siegel decided that "Brad Pitt reeks charisma. In an excellent performance, he has Oscar-nominee potential."

For the most part, the critics might as well not have bothered to write about Brad. They were irrelevant. The audiences knew what they wanted, and they wanted him. Along the line that had taken him from *A River Runs Through It* to *Legends of the Fall* he'd grown into something that went beyond mere movie stardom. Nor was it as simple as just being a heartthrob. Women of all ages, types and backgrounds loved him. Some wanted to sleep with him, some wanted to mother him, others wanted to know all about him.

No one had engineered it. It was a phenomenon. Brad Pitt had quietly become the man who'd entranced female America and more. There were fans in Britain, Europe—everywhere his movies had been released.

His popularity was simply a testament to the animal magnetism he possessed. Charisma—no one else had had it in the same way for a long time. It was the thing that made stars into screen legends and popular icons.

In *Legends of the Fall,* the story, and the character of Tristan, showed just how much of it was in Brad. To be sure, Tristan's romantic side was quite deliberately played up—in an essentially conservative family he was the wild one with long golden hair when the others were brunette, and he wore loose, free clothing while they were confined in their suits—but the crowds believed Brad in the role every bit as much as he believed himself in it.

He was so immersed that he was able to add things that weren't in the script, which were just right, completely in character.

Aidan Quinn noted in *Premiere*, "I happened onto some dailies that were on tape, and saw him at that grave, and he was just devastating. Brad's got a very traditional, manly kind of persona, so to see that man fighting the emotion and not winning—there was stuff he was adding that wasn't scripted—was just so powerful, watching it spill out."

It was beyond craft. This was pure instinct. As Tristan, Brad enjoyed the magic of the perfect actor in the perfect part. He'd been born to do this. The emotions Tristan felt, the conflicts and anguish, radiated out of him to the camera. He might have been a man of few words, but really, he hardly needed any. Marshall Herskovitz, the movie's producer, told Brad, even before filming began, "You have the luxury here to feel as much as you want," and Brad had taken the advice to heart. In return he'd given an outstanding performance. The film had been much more to him than another script, another job, and it showed.

Legends of the Fall appeared in theaters just a month after *Interview with the Vampire,* and its timing could hardly have been better. The world had a chance to see the full range of Brad's acting skills. In many ways Louis and Tristan could not have been farther apart—one seeking death, the other searching for redemption—yet there was a thread of desperation, then resignation, that linked them both. But they remained, quite literally, night and day.

With two major releases so close together, and the amount written about each of them, it almost seemed as if America was in the midst of a Brad Pitt glut. His face and name were on billboards and posters everywhere, to the point where it seemed impossible not to know who he was. A Golden Globe nomination for his work as Tristan—the movie garnered another; neither won—only cemented the impression.

In the end, what could have been overkill worked in his favor. It sent him over the top in terms of popularity. After seeing both films almost back to back, the effect of Brad was devastating. He was already a movie star; now he was a household name.

The idea that Brad was everywhere was only heightened when a cover story about him appeared in *Rolling Stone* to coincide with the release of *Interview with the Vampire.* That issue was snapped up like ice cream in August, as was *Vanity Fair,* a few weeks later, when it, too, featured Brad on the cover.

What exactly was going on? There seemed to be an outbreak of Brad mania in the country.

It was understandable, really. He was more visible than he'd ever been before, with starring roles in two of the biggest box office movies. Between them, they showed him to be sexy, sensitive, gorgeous, and filled with presence.

A number of people had discovered him earlier, with *Thelma & Louise* or *A River Runs Through It.* But the end of 1994 marked his mass breakthrough. Almost everybody wanted to know about Brad Pitt, and even the ones who didn't knew who he was.

If it all seemed like it was lurching out of control, the whirlwind had barely begun. Every year, in mid-January, *People* named its choice for "The Sexiest Man Alive." In 1995 they showed themselves in tune with the pulse of America, picking Brad.

It wasn't a contest—just plain fact. At the time

there was nobody even remotely close. Needless to say, copies swept off the newsstands almost as fast as they could be stacked. He'd been given, in a way, the official seal of approval.

So, suddenly, Brad *was* everywhere. The television tabloid entertainment and news shows were carrying stories about him, he was the feature of gossip columns, he was photographed at events and clubs. Every single move he made was scrutinized.

"This last year," Brad told journalist Johanna Schneller, "I've been as happy as I've ever been, been miserable, been genius, been humiliated, been congratulated, been put down—I mean the whole gamut of emotions. That's a pretty amazing year."

And it had been amazing. He'd taken his time, and eased into the last stretch towards super stardom almost reluctantly, but once his decision had been made, he'd dived straight in and fully embraced it.

But, try as he might, he couldn't become comfortable with the notion of himself as a star. He was an actor, an artist, a worker, not a pinup. He still had favorite actors, people whose work he really admired and who he tried to emulate, but he did not see them as idols. Not in the way people looked at him. It just didn't seem right to him, somehow, to think of anyone that way, most especially him. He knew his own faults and quirks all too well. How could anyone idolize him?

But they did. What was happening was virtually unprecedented. Brad's popularity was continuing to spiral. The ones who read *People,* who'd been unfamiliar with his work before, decided to investigate. It kept *Legends of the Fall* doing a roaring business.

America hadn't had a star like this in a generation. Perhaps the last comparable example had been Robert Redford, who achieved the pinnacle of his fame in the early 1970s.

Brad's appeal wasn't limited to any single age-group. From thirteen to eighty, women were attracted to him. For the young, part of it was the long hair and the goattee he'd grown, which marked him as one of them. Others ignored that, and saw the lovely planes of his face, the torso, the gentlemanly manner. He became the fantasy object of teenagers, their mothers, and sometimes even their grandmothers!

Even lesbians like singing star Melissa Etheridge weren't immune to his appeal.

"He could change a woman's mind," she admitted.

It had gone well past temporary fascination with an idol, or even the idea of a heartthrob. Brad had already been both of those. This was, it seemed, almost universal. Women simply loved him.

At the same time, men didn't resent him, which was quite a rarity. But certainly it was understandable. The roles Brad played were, for the most part manly and physical—breaking wild horses, plunging through a river. Like many men, his characters didn't discuss their emotions. They could relate to him.

Brad had gifts they envied, but it was impossible to hate him for it because of the way he accepted his gifts. To him, those gifts were just there. He didn't make a big deal of them, or try to hide them; they just existed, and he got on with his life.

But his life, of course, kept changing. Going out to see a band, or just hanging out and drinking a few beers in a club wasn't as easy as it once had been. Not when his face was everywhere—on movie posters, in magazines, on television, in peoples' minds. Being so well known should have made things better; instead he found his options for fun becoming more and more limited.

So mostly he stayed home, putting his new house in order. When he did venture out, it was to places like the Viper Room, owned by movie star Johnny Depp, where Brad could find a table in the shadows, smoke his Camels, and drink his beer without being bothered. There was the House of Blues, often full of celebrities from films and music, where he could join others in similar positions, such as R.E.M.'s singer, Michael Stipe, who just wanted to be able to hear music without being hassled.

Brad had always been a Hollywood outsider, not part of any "brat pack," not socializing with other actors of his own age. Now, with time, he decided to try and discover them, and get to know the people who were doing the same kind of work as himself. But it proved to be a disappointing, futile exercise.

"I met a bunch of people," he complained, "and it was that whole competitive, look-over, high-school-cafeteria thing. It was a shame. What's with that?"

Nor was he in favor of the substance abuse that seemed endemic among his contemporaries who were trying to be cool. It had, after all, helped kill River Phoenix.

"I've seen a lot of young actors go through that," Brad said in *Movieline,* talking about drugs. "They think they'll lose their creativity going straight. So many people—*I* even had the notion that you had to be miserable to be great. But then you gotta say, well, why does everyone either die from drugs, or quit? So how good can it be? Very simple question. Very tough answer. I don't trust drugs."

Young Hollywood was visible, had money and power, but it didn't impress him.

"Well, don't you wonder where the young Pacinos, the young DeNiros, the young Walkens, the young Duvalls, the young Newmans, the young Redfords are?" he asked. "Who do we have now that's young and inspiring? . . . I wanna see that collection of young guys get strong. I'd like to be inspired again. Let's see some intelligence. I don't see a lot of intelligence with the young people, you know?"

Not walking with the crowd, being willing to take chances, approaching his acting intelligently—those had become Brad's hallmarks, and he saw no reason to change them now. He needed to keep stretching himself, testing his limits as an actor; that was the only way to keep improving, and to not end up stale.

That was one reason he refused to sign for the movie version of Scott Smith's book, *A Simple Plan*. After filming *Interview with the Vampire*, he had no wish to follow it up with another depressing movie.

So instead he took a co-starring role in *Seven*, a very straight-ahead police drama/thriller. In it he was set to play a young cop, the partner to Morgan Freeman's closer-to-retirement character, on the trail of a serial killer whose murders are tied to the seven deadly sins.

"The guy's got no problems, that's the key thing," Brad said of his role as a police officer. "It's been a blast so far."

But if it was fun all the way, it would have been too easy. Brad injured his hand during the shooting, leaving him wearing a cast when he was not actually in front of the cameras.

That was bad enough, but the filming also necessitated a huge change in Brad's appearance—the long hair, which had been there since he finished work on *A River Runs Through It*, and which had become one of his most identifiable features, had to go.

Once it was done and he'd adjusted to the new look, he realized that he was happy with it; it had been time for a change. At least he'd kept the beard—for the moment, anyway. As soon as *Seven* was complete, he was due to begin work on *Twelve Monkeys*, a time travel adventure directed by former Monty Python member Terry Gilliam *(Brazil)*, which would see Brad sharing the screen with Bruce Willis and Madeleine Stowe in a huge epic. How he'll look in that remains to be seen.

After that, there was talk of filming *The Vampire Lestat*, another of Anne Rice's "Vampire Chronicles." *Interview* had been so difficult and draining for Brad that he was willing to appear in this purely because "Louis is only in the next book for about five minutes." And he certainly wouldn't let his hair grow back for the role. That style was over and done with.

"I'd put on a wig," he said.

So Brad seems set for the immediate future. A daunting work schedule, and no shortage of offers, even with an asking price of $6 million a movie. On top of that, the sexiest man alive. Who could ask for more?

Ten

In the long run, what will happen to Brad Pitt? Will he continue to act, gaining stature and, finally, critical acceptance, through a lasting career? That's quite possible. Certainly the demand to see him in films shows no sign of abating. *Legends of the Fall* grossed $60 million in the first two months of its release, largely on the basis of Brad's performance, while *Interview with the Vampire* proved even more popular, bringing in $105 million in three months.

He's reached a rare plateau. Almost anything he does now will draw huge crowds. His appearance in a film is a guarantee of success.

He's worked hard for it, though, and gone his own way, taking the route that seemed right to him, not necessarily the easiest or the shortest road.

He can afford to be selective these days, to take the parts that really appeal. The scripts that choke his mailbox every day are the very best Hollywood can offer.

But will it be enough for Brad?

That remains to be seen. But it's not out of the question that he'll go the same way as the person he's often been compared to—Robert Redford. Redford still acts occasionally, but in the last few years has acquired a greater reputation as a director of quality cinema—*A River Runs Through It* and *Quiz Show,* for example.

As far back in his career as *Thelma & Louise,* Brad had shown inclinations to bring projects of his own to the screen—in that case a movie about Chet Baker. And his involvement in *Legends of the Fall* went beyond his acting. So it may well be that Brad will want to try his own hand at directing sometime in the future. It wouldn't really come as a surprise, given that he's been known to criticize the "cheesiness" of the way some of his films have ended up. He'd probably like to have that control, to be able to maintain the integrity of a project, even if it meant bucking the system.

For now he's on his way to becoming an actor without compare in his age group. Brad has it all—the looks, the ability, the desire not be pigeonholed or labeled. He's unwilling to coast on his success and make a career out of being a celebrity. He has to keep trying, pushing himself to find those little "perfect moments."

"Don't have many," he said, "but that's what keeps you going. Because they're all over the place, just hard to find. There's this bag for perfect moments that you carry around with you. And then when you find them, occasionally, and add to the bag, you really appreciate it."

The idea may sound rather Zen, but then, that's the way Brad lives. He may look to the future and think about the past, but his real concentration is on the present, the now.

Since splitting up with Jitka Pohlodek, he's been spotted with a number of different women. He dated actress Uma Thurman, and exchanged Valentine's Day cards with rock star Courtney Love, the widow of Nirvana's Kurt Cobain, but neither relationship has seemed at all serious. The most recent reports have him involved with his co-star from *Seven,* Gwyneth Paltrow, but that was denied by everyone concerned, who deemed them the usual "just good friends," although, once the filming was complete, they seemed to become fairly constant companions, spotted sharing kisses, and even travelling to Europe together for the premiere of *Legends of the Fall.*

He's learned, from his time with Juliette and Yit, that he's not ready to settle down just yet. Both his brother and sister have done it—and had kids—but Brad has an independent streak that seems to have bypassed them. He loved Juliette, and their three years together were wonderful—for both of them—but now it's space that he needs, a lack of involvement, and time to fully find himself before he does make any romantic commitment.

But that's perfectly natural. He's in a situation that's far from normal. He can't live in the usual way. At one time he'd found that it was easy to disappear in Los Angeles and just be anonymous, but these days his face has become so familiar that it's virtually impossible. The idea of going to the grocery store or out for a pizza has become little more than a dream. Only at night, in the clubs where other celebrities hang out, can Brad have anything like a normal life.

That's partly why he treasures his house so much. It's a refuge, a place he can tend to, where friends can come and stay, where he can really be himself, play his music loud, watch trashy movies on cable until dawn, and relax. It's not like most bachelor places, though. Once he'd moved in and arranged things the way he wanted them, the place was neat and shining, the wood polished, the dishes done. As long as he had money he'd been collecting antiques, and here he could show them off to perfection. An old tube radio, Depression glass, and Tiffany, old farm ware—all were lovingly displayed. The only thing not in exquisite order was his large collection of CDs, randomly stacked in one of the house's original glass-front cabinets. And that, he explained was because "you're on the search. You just find the right one for the needed moment."

The Zen ideas creep in everywhere in his life.

He still hasn't completely come to terms with his fame. When he's on the set he's a complete professional, but away from it there are plenty of other things he'd rather be doing than acting. Brad would still love to be a musician. They're *his* idols—the late Stevie Ray Vaughn, the Doors, Marianne Faithful—the people he looks up to. He still plays, although strictly for pleasure. One of his bedrooms contains guitars, recording equipment, almost everything he'd need to record an album—not that he ever will. Thoughts and dreams of being a musician might linger in his mind, but he knows enough people in the business now to understand what's involved; he couldn't give it the time it would need for success. Still, music remains, as it has been since he first heard Elton John on the radio, one of the real joys in his life.

So does art. The teenager who carried a notebook and pencil with him to be able to draw has become the adult who takes a sketchbook everywhere. He still loves architecture, particularly the work of Charles Rennie Mackintosh, the man who designed many of the buildings in Glasgow. Brad has even been trying his own hand at design, in his case dark, Gothic-style furniture. He's even considered opening a small furniture store in Los Angeles to sell them.

That may or may not happen. But the love of art and music will certainly never die within him.

Sooner or later the critics will take him seriously. So far acknowledgments of his work have seemed grudging, as if the reviewers were astonished that he was capable of a powerful performance. It's as if his looks have worked against him there, that someone so handsome couldn't possibly have acting ability. Yet again and again, Brad's proven that he can give depth to a fairly superficial character, or make a complex one understandable.

That gift is rare. Even rarer is the power to make both seem completely natural. Many actors are good at the great scene, at portraying the extremes of emotion, the histrionics, shouting, crying, laughing. Brad's greatest power as an actor is to be able to show all those in the way normal people do, in a generally understated manner, keeping much of it within, and letting it show in small ways, through the eyes and face and in small gestures.

But more than that, it's his charisma that's pulled him into the limelight. The camera and the eye both love him. There's simply no choice but to focus on him. Having seen him, viewers can't help but remember him. Whether it's his face, his smile, his physique, or just his sheer presence, he stays in the mind and the heart.

These days Brad sells. A story about him in a magazine is a guarantee of increased sales. His picture on a cover, even a mention of him there, is certain to pull people in. When *Newsweek* ran a story about the way America was dressing down, the center of the cover was Brad in an old sweater, with his long hair and goattee. Never mind that he barely warranted a mention in the article, his presence was more than enough to make people stop and take notice. Reportedly though, after the article appeared, Brad went out and spent $15,000 on new clothes. Even the *National Enquirer* gave a full page to his history as "Hollywood's Number One Heartbreaker," which might well have been something of an exaggeration, but made for great copy. In truth, he's had fewer relationships and dated far less women than most other men in his position. That might seem odd, given that so many women would willingly drop everything to go out with him. But he's a romantic; he's still searching for the person who can be as special to him as Juliette was. It seemed right with Yit for a while, but the timing was bad—on the rebound, in the middle of such a hectic filming schedule. It was impossible, destined to fail.

Any woman he's seen with these days will generate rumors of a new relationship. And sooner or later, they'll be right. But for the moment, as he keeps a very tight focus on his career, it seems as if Brad won't have the time for serious entanglements.

By his own admission, Brad's had a very easy life. He's drifted, let things wash over him and carry him along. It's an unusual way to reach superstardom; most of the people who achieve it are driven, intense souls. For Brad, laid back, relaxed about the whole thing, taking the jobs he found stimulating, the idea of success is quite funny, almost a cosmic joke. It never mattered that much to him—which is probably why it happened. Mention it and you'll get a grin and a slight shake of his head.

There's far too much of the gentle southern boy in there for that to ever change. What Brad shows to the public—his reticence, his charm, his politeness—is all real. Everything goes back to the way Bill and Jane Pitt raised their children in Springfield. Good manners, a secure sense of self, and humility—these were good lessons to learn in life. They've helped keep his feet very firmly on the ground when the craziness of Hollywood, and people telling him how great he was, could have swept him away. The shotgun he keeps, the one his father gave him when he was a boy, serves as more than a deterrent to intruders; it's a very tangible link to his past.

Will Brad's popularity ever fade? Will he become a has-been, a character actor who pops up here and there, in films and television, eking out a living in small roles? No. He's gone too far. Hunks and babes come and go, and he's certainly been classed as one, but he's too big for that ever to happen. Overnight successes become overnight failures all the time, but that's not the way Brad's career has been. He's made his mark slowly, but far more firmly. It might not have been the orthodox way, but it's worked. He's become part of the American culture of the nineties. Naming him "The Sexiest Man Alive" simply put the seal on the package, and confirmed what so many people had been saying for a few years.

Sure, there'll be plenty of younger, good-looking actors coming along—there already are—some of them with real talent. A few among them will stay the course. But Brad is established. He has a unique position. He's exactly what America has wanted for a generation, a movie star in the old tradition—charismatic, charming, dashingly handsome, romantic, and a consummate actor—a combination of Gable, Dean, and Redford.

That will keep him going. Where it will lead him remains to be seen. But he'll follow his instincts and do exactly what he wants. That much is certain. It'll be a journey that'll never be less than interesting, a future as rewarding as the past.

In the eyes of *People,* his time as "The Sexiest Man Alive" will pass. But for those who've come to love him through his films, it'll be the title he'll carry for the rest of his life.

And to Brad? Well, he'll just keep on living his life, with a smile and a shake of his head.